SQUADRON A
AN INFORMAL HISTORY OF ITS SECOND HALF-CENTURY OF SERVICE

A Sequel to the History of Its First Fifty Years

by
Edward L. Bimberg

Authorized by the Squadron A Foundation

ROBERT U. WHITNEY, Jr., Chairman, Board of Directors
ROBERT L. McLEAN, President
GEORGE A. RENTSCHLER, Vice-President
BENJAMIN B. McALPIN III, Vice-President
LOGAN FULRATH, Jr., Secretary/Adj.
MICHAEL WITTER, Treasurer
HARRIET HUEBSCH, Executive Director

EAGLE EDITIONS
2005

EAGLE EDITIONS
AN IMPRINT OF HERITAGE BOOKS, INC.

Books, CDs, and more – Worldwide

For our listing of thousands of titles see our website at

www.HeritageBooks.com

Published 2005 by
HERITAGE BOOKS, INC.
Publishing Division
65 East Main Street
Westminster, Maryland 21157-5026

COPYRIGHT © 2005 THE SQUADRON A FOUNDATION

All rights reserved. No part of this book may be reproduced or transmitted in any form or by any means, electronic or mechanical, including photocopying, recording or by any information storage and retrieval system without written permission from the author, except for the inclusion of brief quotations in a review.

International Standard Book Number: **0-7884-3504-3**

THE EXECUTIVE COMMITTEE OF SQUADRON A

Chairman: Benjamin B. McAlpin III

Arthur Armitage, Samuel N. Benjamin, Henry L. Collins III, George J. Dotsey, Logan Fulrath, Jr., Charles A. Harris, James B. Horton, Vincent A. Katinas, Robert L. McLean, George A. Rentschler, Michael D. Witter

CONTENTS

Introduction vii
Chapter 1. Prologue 1
Chapter 2. The Path Toward War 7
Chapter 3. At Last—Combat! 29
Chapter 4. Home From The Wars 37
Chapter 5. The Big Move 51
Chapter 6. Across The Bay 65

Appendices
   Appendix I. Roster of Squadron A Officers (January 27, 1941) 71
   Appendix II. "With the 101st Cavalry In World War II" 73
   Appendix III. Horse Activities Program, 1949-1950 129
   Appendix IV. "Answering the 9-11 Call" 137

Squadron A Members 147
2004 Officers 157
Addendum 161

INTRODUCTION

THIS is the story of the *second* fifty years of Squadron A. The history of the National Guard cavalry unit has paralleled that of the City of New York for a colorful and exciting century of service to that city, the State of New York and the nation.

The military organization that began so long ago as Squadron A has at various times in its history become part of the 101st Cavalry of the New York National Guard (amongst other designations) and has been known to the members of the Squadron A Association as "the active unit." Today the active unit is officially the 1st Battalion, 101st Cavalry (Tank), with its headquarters and two companies on Staten Island, and three companies stationed in upstate New York. We honor its members and respect them as our spiritual descendants, considering their history indistinguishable from our own. You will also find in our story considerable reference to Squadron C. This was the Brooklyn Units of the 101st Cavalry, as Squadron A was known as the Manhattan Units. They, too, are part of our history.

The activities of the *first* fifty years of Squadron A have been recorded in a volume of memoirs originally published in 1939. We respectfully continue from there. But, as a first chapter, we present a brief review of that initial half-century.

–THE SQUADRON A ASSOCIATION

CHAPTER 1. PROLOGUE

IN the latter part of the nineteenth century most well-born young men in America rode pleasure horses. In spite of their urban background, New York City's "swells" were no exception. In 1884 a group of youthful men-about-Manhattan formed themselves into a mounted social club to engage in the political rallies and parades that were a part of the Blaine-Cleveland presidential campaign of that year. The club backed Blaine. He lost, but some 18 of its members stuck together and carried on with their mounted organization.

Perhaps because the memories of Civil War horrors had by this time receded and young men were once again drawn to the glories of war, the newly founded organization gave itself a military twist. It was now called the "New York Hussars" and was eventually outfitted in colorful dress uniforms–sky blue hussar jackets braided in black, with striped breeches to match. Headgear was a black fur busby with yellow trim and a perky black plume, all very dashing.

It was the beginnings of a remarkable National Guard cavalry regiment that became the center of equestrian activities in New York City and remained that way for more than half a century. Even today its traditions are kept alive by a National Guard tank unit called the 101st Cavalry and by a social organization with military and equestrian interests still known as Squadron A.

The Hussars continued to lend a colorful air to the New York scene with their presence at parades and other gatherings around the city. They invited additional select young men to join the Hussars (bring your own horse or rent one from the local riding academy), and the original 18 expanded to 40-odd, all of whom apparently thought rather well of themselves. They even had the nerve to send formal invitations to prominent senior Regular Army officers, including William Tecumseh Sherman himself, to become an "Honorary Member of the First Hussars of New York." Amazingly, all of these high ranking officers accepted, although there is no record that any of them took part in the troop's activities, or even visited it, for that matter.

Except for General Sherman, who in 1887 was guest of honor at a First Hussars' dinner at Delmonico's, then the trendiest restaurant in town.

In 1888 a Lieutenant Charles F. Roe, recently resigned from the Regular Army cavalry after 20 years of service with a distinguished record in the Indian Wars, joined the Hussars. He soon became captain and commanding officer, and under his inspired leadership things changed. Apparently the infusion of old Indian fighter blood was just what the effete New Yorkers needed. The playboy image of the Hussars was submerged under strict military discipline—and unlikely as it seemed at the time, the men loved it. The silk-stocking parade soldiers became real, if only part-time, cavalrymen.

Captain Roe now felt that the time had come for the Hussars to join the *bona fide* military establishment. He applied to the state capital at Albany and on April 2, 1889 the New York Hussars, 51 men strong, officially became Troop A of the National Guard of the State of New York.

The parades and parties continue, however, but now the Troop was subject to call-ups for riot duty in that era of turbulent labor disputes. There were the famous Brooklyn trolley riots of 1895 and a railroad strike in Buffalo in 1892 for which the Troop turned out. There was never any serious fighting in these conflicts; the mere appearance of men on horseback seemed to discourage even the most enthusiastic rioter.

By the time the Spanish-American War broke out in 1898 Troop A had been expanded to three troops and become Squadron A. Since the government apparently couldn't afford to mobilize the entire Squadron and its horses, volunteers were selected from each troop for active service in that "splendid little war." Not that it made much difference; by the time the provisional troop from Squadron A reached Puerto Rico the war was virtually over. Its only wartime duty was to ride out under a flag of truce to notify the Spanish officers that there was to be no more fighting and to investigate rumors that Spanish soldiers had massacred local residents. The charge could not be confirmed and the troopers rode back to their camp at Ponce. In a few weeks they were back in Manhattan and were part-time soldiers once again.

While settling down to its peacetime routine, Squadron A maintained its sporting flavor. In the latter part of the century James Gordon Bennett brought polo from Great Britain to the United States.

This was right up the alley of the gentlemen troopers, and by 1904 Squadron A polo teams were playing the galloping game on Long Island, in Westchester and in New York City's Van Cortlandt Park. The polo tradition of Squadron A. was one that lasted through two World Wars.

In 1916 when the Mexican revolutionary, Pancho Villa, started raiding across the border, President Wilson once again called up the National Guard. The squadron was now 500 strong, but there was a shortage of horses. Finally, after much confusion, suitable (and some not so suitable) mounts were obtained and the troopers and their horses entrained for Texas.

While the regular army cavalry under General John J. Pershing chased Villa deep into Mexico, the National Guard patrolled the border. It was no picnic. The troops were plagued by desert conditions–alternatively drought and floods, flying insects, tarantulas, scorpions and rattlesnakes. All the while a strict military regimen was maintained, with long, tough patrols, continuous firing practice and frequent inspections. The latter were considered a bore, but of all the cavalry along the border, Squadron A received the highest rating of any National Guard unit in federal service.

This time a great many of the Squadron's enlisted men were either released for officer training or commissioned in the unit itself. The missing ranks were soon refilled and the Squadron was brought up to full war strength. The fighting in Europe had proven that the machine gun was the master of the battlefield, and Squadron A arrived in France newly designated as the 105th Machine Gun Battalion. Its horses were used as mounts for the officers and for the "runners," the mounted messengers who were the principal means of military communications in a mobile situation before the advent of the radio–some of the horses ended up in draft, pulling the battalion's supply carts. These were augmented by army mules, which the men called "Tennessee canaries."

By the end of July 1918 the battalion was in Belgium in the thick of the fighting. Assigned to the British Second Army, it took part in breaking the Hindenberg Line and by October was fighting the retreating Germans along the Selle River. Casualties were heavy in all these engagements and by the time the war was over the 105th had earned its share of battle honors.

Even throughout the horror of mud and blood that was World War I, Squadron A always seemed to be cultivating its "silk stocking" image. There is a story, perhaps apocryphal, of the Squadron's arrival at the front. A young Squadron lieutenant, booted and spurred and immaculately turned out, was asked what his mission was. "Our mission," he replied, "is to lend a little *éclat* to what would otherwise be a rather vulgar affair!"

The decade after World War I was known as the Roaring Twenties– and Squadron A roared right along with it. The armory, besides being headquarters for serious military training, also became something of a pleasure palace, with polo games, horse shows, parties and dances among the activities. The polo team was reborn and a horse show team created. The latter, in just a few seasons of showing, won more than 200 ribbons in shows throughout Long Island, Westchester and Connecticut.

The social life of Squadron A continued right into the 1930s, and every Saturday night the tanbark drill floor of the 94th Street Armory resounded to the pounding of hooves and the shouts of players and spectators as the Squadron team competed against a variety of civilian and military teams.

A 1936 ticket to the Saturday night double-headers revealed that on that particular evening at 8:30 the Gypsy Polo Club played Governor's Island, and at 9:30 Squadron A played Winged Foot (the New York Athletic Club team). General admission was 50 cents, reserved seats $1. After the game there was a dance for members and their guests– admission $1 and evening dress was required. Music was supplied by Stanley Melba's orchestra, then the most popular "society" orchestra in New York.

But the period of the 1930s had begun with an economic turndown that became known as the Great Depression, and although that didn't interfere very much with the social life of Squadron A, worse was to come. The decade was to end with a war in Europe.

HERE TWO TROOPERS ENJOY ONE OF THE MANY SOCIAL OCCASIONS WHEN THE DRESS UNIFORM WAS CONSIDERED *DE RIGEUER*. THE SCENE APPEARS TO BE "EL MOROCCO," ONE OF MANHATTAN'S TRENDIEST NIGHT SPOTS OF THE 1930S-40S ERA.

THE ARMORY

A SQUADRON A POLO TEAM OF THE 1930S.
(L TO R) ZENAS COLT, BILL SHILLABER, COBBLES STURHAHN.
THE SATURDAY NIGHT POLO GAMES WERE A HIGHLIGHT
OF THE NEW YORK SOCIAL SCENE.

CHAPTER 2. THE PATH TOWARD WAR

NEW YORK CITY in the late 1930s was for most New Yorkers (and for a great many others) the Center of the Universe, the Crossroads of the World. It had the world's tallest office tower, fabulous Broadway shows, wonderful museums and art galleries, a financial capital on Wall Street almost recovered from the crash of '29, a Harlem Renaissance, one could go on and on. It also had a few corrupt politicians and crooked cops. It was, indeed, still O'Henry's "Baghdad on the Subway."

And it still had horses. In spite of the plethora of motor vehicles and the burgeoning traffic problems, the horse was a noticeable fact of life in Manhattan. There were a half dozen or so riding academies, most of them located on the west side near the park, but at least one on the east side. This was the colorful Boots and Saddles Riding Club, with a tiny indoor ring, operated by three former Czarist Russian cavalry officers, including a Circassian prince. And patient draft horses still delivered the milk throughout the city.

And then there was Squadron A. It had no Circassian princes, but it did have a huge, block-long drill shed with a tanbark floor and extensive facilities for horses. It had a squadron of National Guard horse cavalry (minus enough horses to make it ineffectual without borrowing some in an emergency). It had exciting polo games open to the public every Saturday night and a Spring Horse Show that was said to be the biggest and most popular indoor show, after the National at Madison Square Garden. And although Europe was sliding faster and faster toward war, America as a whole was hardly conscious of the menace. New York City, however, was something of an exception. For at that time, in spite of the machinations of the "let's stay out of it" America First movement and the blatantly pro-Hitler German-American Bund, there was strong sympathy for the British.

But little thought of this coming war was on the minds of the troopers of Squadron A as they continued their polo and parties and weekly military training in the armory. The gravity of the situation only began to sink in as the time for summer camp approached, when it became apparent that the fun and games of the normal two weeks summer encampment at Pine Camp was not to be repeated in 1939. Instead, there would be deadly serious maneuvers in upstate New York, in the vicinity of Plattsburg.

The Plattsburg Maneuvers were destined to be rough on Squadron A and the entire 101st Cavalry. The first week, however, was not unlike previous encampments with the days devoted to the usual settling in, minor tactical exercises and one overnight bivouac. Nights were like old times with singing around the campfire, and a certain amount of drinking. The favorite beverage was called "Gingaboo" (subject to change of name and spelling from troop to troop) which was the contribution of a portion of each trooper's liquor poured into one large pot and quaffed in canteen cups. It's a wonder anyone survived.

But the second week was different. It was the toughest of maneuvers on a large scale with an under-equipped 101st Cavalry, of generally unfit city boys suffering all the discomforts of actual combat; heat, extreme fatigue of both man and beast, hunger and thirst, sleeplessness–but without the ultimate horror of being shot at. Luckily the whole business lasted only two weeks.

Major Frederick T. (Fritz) Vietor who commanded the 2nd Squadron (Squadron A) in these maneuvers wrote a detailed account of the Squadron's part in them, as a supplement to the history of the first fifty years. A principal theme in his account is the value of horse cavalry, even in this age of mechanization, pointing out every instance throughout the maneuvers where the mounted soldier proved superior to his mechanized cousin. In one instance he describes how units of the 101st Cavalry, charging down hill and jumping a stone wall, so surprised an enemy force that it scattered and ran without firing a shot. He also relates how Troop K captured Brigadier General Walter C. Short, commanding the 1st Infantry Division. (Who could have known that a few years hence that same general would be commanding in Hawaii–and be blamed for the debacle at Pearl Harbor?

In spite of Major Vietor's encomium for horse cavalry, the reader can find between the lines a story that tells of the weakness of the cavalry arm, particularly when ranged against tanks and artillery. The major's last sentence reads, "The general feeling was that we had done a good job and that the horse cavalry as a whole had not suffered because of our operations."

Apparently not everyone agreed. Although there is no question that the officers and men of Squadron A and, indeed, of the entire 101st Cavalry worked hard and skillfully and demonstrated the highest *esprit de corps*, the results of the Plattsburg maneuvers did little to slow the eventual mechanization of the cavalry arm. Colonel Charles A. "Chuck" Graydon, a Squadron C lieutenant at the time, whose platoon was attached to Major Vietor's unit in the maneuvers, later wrote, "The 101st Cavalry had its own sad experience with mechanized forces in the 1939 First Army maneuvers at Plattsburg, N.Y. Faced against the Provisional Armored Corps, it was no match for such an organization. To many young cavalrymen 'the handwriting was on the wall.'"

Regardless, the experiences of the Squadron in the Plattsburg maneuvers was a beneficial one as far as training was concerned and the men learned a little more about real war. That information would be needed in the not too distant future, for just a few weeks after the Squadron's return from camp the Germans invaded Poland. The previous year, when the British and French had capitulated to Hitler in the matter of the Nazi takeover in Czechoslovakia, Winston Churchill had remarked, "The government had to choose between shame and war. They chose shame and they will get war." He was right.

The opening of hostilities in Europe pushed the United States a little further down the road toward the brink. The armory drills became more serious, and while the America Firsters still railed about keeping the U.S. out of the European conflict, there was no doubt that the mood of the country was becoming more sympathetic to the Allied cause.

There was to be one more summer encampment of Squadron A before the 101st Cavalry was called into federal service in preparation for World War II. In 1940 the regiment was once again engaged in maneuvers, this time with a base camp at a ghost town called Pyrites near Canton, N.Y. Sometimes known as "fool's gold," pyrite is a useful mineral formerly mined in the area. Apparently the vein had run out and there were just a few broken down houses left to remind the troopers that a town had once existed there.

For Squadron A the maneuvers followed the pattern of that of the previous summer, with the usual hard riding, sweat, dust, missed meals and sleeplessness, interspersed with a few half-hearted campfire parties. A monograph written after the war Colonel Graydon, from memory, paints a colorful picture of the 101st Cavalry in its last encampment as a fully mounted unit:

> The long line of cavalry slowly wound its way westward through softly rolling country toward the setting sun. The entire column could be seen intermittently as it crested hills and then partially disappeared at the lower elevations.
>
> The colonel commanding rode at the head of the column closely followed by the national and regimental colors, side by side. Behind, the red and white troop guidons flapped in the breeze at intervals down the line. The only sounds were those of cavalry in motion—creaking saddle leather, jingle of curb chains, the faint rattle of mess kits and the muffled sound of hooves as they struck the ground, accented by sharper noises as they glanced off rocks.
>
> Each trooper wore the campaign hat with yellow hat cord, khaki shirt and breeches, boots and spurs. A Colt .45 cal. automatic hung at his belt. On each McClellan saddle hung his saddle bags, bed roll and raincoat. Each horse wore the cavalry bit and bridoon bridle and a halter with halter shank. A Springfield model 1903 rifle hung in its scabbard on the horse's near side. The Phillips pack saddles of the machine gun platoon of each rifle troop carried the Browning light machine gun while those of the machine gun troop carried the water-cooled heavy machine gun.
>
> It was a sight to excite the mind of every cavalryman. This was not a scenario for a western. It was a firsthand description of the 101st Cavalry during its last field training exercise before going into federal service. The time was August 1940 and the place upper New York State near the little town of Canton. Many there had a premonition that they would never see a full regiment of cavalry on the march again.

And they never did. When the squadron returned to Manhattan from the 1940 maneuvers they found that although the war in Europe had been going on for almost a year the city (and the country) was just now beginning to wake up to the danger America was in.

The signs in Squadron A were small but noticeable. The drill periods were longer and more serious, the parties fewer and – horrors! – there was no more polo.

Then the government under President Franklin D. Roosevelt called the entire National Guard, some 300,000 men, into federal service. There was a big shakeup in the guard cavalry regiments. The 101st was scheduled to be federalized on January 27, 1941, and was simultaneously reorganized as a "horse-mechanized" regiment, with one squadron remaining horsed and the other mechanized.

As that fateful day of federalization approached, the activity in the armory increased. Men came and went at all hours of the day and far into the evening. Weapons were checked and double-checked, horses were vetted and saddles repaired. Uniforms were pressed, boots polished and spurs shined. Sometimes the spit-and-polish was overdone, as when a few eager beavers applied a currently popular liquid polish called "Dyanshine" to their boots and then set the boots afire with a match. The hoped-for result was a beautiful burned-in shine—but if you didn't blow out the flame quickly enough there could be a disaster!

The men settled their business affairs and older, married men were released. Last minute recruiting was carried out with the aim of signing up the type of men the squadron wanted before the others were thrust upon it. The recruiting drive was successful because it worked both ways; the new recruits could join a crack cavalry regiment with people they knew, or else run the risk of being drafted into some other unit of total strangers. The selective service law was not in force, and it made the search for recruits that much easier.

At last, on a cold evening in early February, the squadron entrained for Fort Devens, Massachusetts, the horses loaded on cattle cars and the men in coaches. It was a long, uncomfortable trip with what was to become a familiar "hurry up and wait" series of unexplained halts, backings and switches—in other words, a typical rail journey of the World War II era. The men took it all in good spirits as an interesting adventure. After all, the U.S. wasn't at war and, according to the law, guard units were only supposed to be in federal service for a year. In 12 short months the men of Squadron A would be back in little old New York for more parties and polo. Or so they thought—ah, the innocence of youth!

Fort Devens was located near Ayer, Massachusetts, a small town a few miles northwest of Boston. When the 101st Cavalry arrived it was *cold* and there was a heavy layer of snow on the ground. The men were prepared for the frigid weather, however, with long overcoats, woolen scarves and heavy sweaters. There was also headgear of a type known to supply sergeants as "cap, winter," a canvas hat with wool lining and ear flaps. Footwear consisted of civilian type galoshes worn over the regular lace-up cavalry boots, a combination that was unsightly but serviceable, and soon many of the officers were wearing waterproof civilian hunting boots, rather than ruining their beautiful custom-made riding boots in the snow. Nevertheless, the first couple of weeks were made particularly uncomfortable by the severity of the unaccustomed New England winter.

To complicate matters, the wooden, two story, "temporary" barracks for the 101st Cavalry were not yet completed and troops were crowded into those buildings that were. To accommodate everyone, cots were jammed together, head to foot. Predictably, there was an epidemic of head colds. To fight against this "nasal pharyngitis," as the overworked doctors (recently drafted into the regiment) described it, the troopers were ordered to erect their shelter halves between each cot. This semi-isolation seemed to do the trick. Within a short time the epidemic was over and with the completion of the barracks so was the necessity of pup tent precautions.

By this time the troopers were beginning to sort out their new duties according to the tables of organization of a horse-mechanized unit. The regiment now looks like this:

Regimental Headquarters
    Service Troop (from Squadron C, Brooklyn)

1st Squadron (Horse)
    Troop A (from Squadron A, Manhattan)
    Troop B (from 121st Cavalry, upstate New York)
    Troop C (from Squadron C, Brooklyn)

2nd Squadron (Mechanized)
    Troop D (Scout Cars, from Squadron A)
    Troop E (Scout Cars, from Squadron A0
    Troop F (Motorcycles, from Squadron C)

Sometimes a unit was composed of both Squadron A and Squadron C men as, for instance, regimental headquarters. The regimental commander, Colonel Gilbert A. Ackerman was from Squadron C, while the adjutant, Captain Larry Larkin, was a Squadron A man, as was the regimental sergeant major, Buddy Quinn. Similarly, while the 1st Squadron commander was Squadron A's Major Alfred G. "Tubby" Tuckerman, the C.O. of the 1st Squadron's headquarters detachment was Captain George Barker of Squadron C. Despite this diversity in origins, it all functioned smoothly.

The theory behind the horse-mechanized regiment was simple. The main function of cavalry was reconnaissance and the idea was that the mechanized units could scout along the road networks (where one existed) and the horse units could keep up with them by transporting their horses in huge "portee" vans. Then, when they came to a place where the road ended, the horse troopers could unload their mounts and continue on, moving ahead over the roadless terrain, while the motor vehicles found a way around.

To perform its job the horse squadron was supplied with huge tractor-trailers maintained and driven by men of the service troop. (Incidentally, the service troop dispatcher of the horse vans was Sergeant Hugh Carey, who later became governor of the State of New York." The tractors were powerful cab-over-engine affairs and the horses, riders and all of their equipment were carried in the ponderous stock trailers behind. A full squad, eight horses and eight men, were crowded into these monstrosities, with the men riding in an open-air compartment in the forward end of the trailer overlooking the cab. To the New Yorkers it was almost like riding on top of a Fifth Avenue double-decker bus of that era; it was pleasant at times, but perfectly miserable when the weather didn't cooperate.

The horses had it somewhat better. Their part of the trailer was more or less open with a canvas top that could be rolled down when circumstances decreed. When the weather was really bad the men managed to get a scrap of the canvas pulled down over their compartment, but since there were no supports to hold it up, it was a rather uncomfortable arrangement. And on long trips there was often a less than pleasant aroma emanating from the horse compartment.

Since the regiment was an experimental one, there was not yet any military manual for loading horses onto a stock trailer, or at least not one available to the lower ranks, so the men had to invent their own method. After trying out various ways of rushing the horses up the rear ramp, a manner was eventually worked out that got the job done without the initial kicking and squealing–and cursing. Eventually all eight horses could be loaded and unloaded quickly and quietly and in a suitably military manner that satisfied the brass.

Learning the ropes was a bit easier for the mechanized troops. The reconnaissance vehicles were light armored trucks called "scout cars." Their armor was not very thick, and they were quite open, which made them vulnerable to rifle or machine gun fire from above, or to a determined grenade attack. Their armament was usually one .50 caliber machine gun and one .30 caliber machine gun. Fortunately they were replaced by better armed and protected armored cars before the regiment actually went to war. Learning to drive a scout car was not that difficult, however, but riding in one could be almost as uncomfortable as riding in an army horse van.

The heroes of the mechanized troops were the motorcycle riders. Their job was everything from dispatch rider to traffic controller, and their mounts were heavy and hard to handle. In bad weather they were miserably uncomfortable to ride and on slippery roads downright dangerous. They were, mercifully, replaced by jeeps before the regiment went overseas.

These were the days of the unprepared and ill-equipped "broomstick army" and although the 101st at Devens was short scout cars, motorcycles, radios and horses, it was not too badly off. As National Guardsmen between the wars the troopers were used to being in short supply; what little was available for our anemic little army of post-World War I went to the regulars and the guardsmen were left out in the cold. Many a Devens trooper recalled having to buy his own cavalry boots at Macy's; the armory issue to recruits was the old leather-faced canvas leggings of World War I, totally unsuitable for a smart looking regiment like the 101st. And for ceremonial occasions they also had to buy their own yellow dress gloves.

Gradually Uncle Sam supplied more modern equipment. The old Model 1903 Springfield rifle was replaced by the Garand M1 semi-automatic piece, but the World War I model steel helmet remained in use for a very long time. The regulation three-buckle boot, the last riding boot ever issued to the U.S. cavalry, eventually found its way to the Devens troopers and, in time, with saddle soap, Kiwi polish and elbow grease, this rather clumsy looking footwear could be softened and shined to the sleekness demanded by regimental standards. Also dispensed by the supply sergeant were the excellent leather gloves the army officially designated as "gloves, horsehide, riding."

The McClellan saddles of the horse troops were slightly changed from those issued to the Union Army in the Civil War, modified by replacing the old cowboy-type cinch with a more modern buckle girth, and later by removing the leather hood from the wooden stirrups. In addition to the McClellans, a few of the troopers had their own English saddles for off-duty riding, while the officers habitually rode in the regulation Phillips officer's saddle.

By this time some of the distinction between Squadron A and Squadron C had become less noticeable, but a few obvious differences remained. For instance, in the horse units Squadron A men tended to keep the brims of their campaign hats turned down, fore and aft, while in Squadron C the style was "brims up." Also, in Squadron A the metal regimental insignia worn on the uniform was, because of its falcon design, known as "the dickie bird." In Squadron C it was called "the duck." And to both Squadron A and Squadron C men, the upstate troopers of Troop B were known, inevitably, as "the apple knockers." Incidentally, Troop B was the lone cavalry remnant of the National Guard's 121st Cavalry, the country boys from the fox hunting Genesee Valley. When called in federal service the rest of their regiment, poor fellows, had been turned into motorized anti-aircraft artillery.

Probably the last expression of any sort of rivalry between Squadrons A and C was an incident that occurred toward the beginning of the Devens tour. The 1st Squadron was enjoying an unofficial bivouac near the quiet little town of Pepperell, New Hampshire, when after what was apparently an evening of some rather serious drinking, person or persons unknown (but probably from Troop C) let a few of Troop A's horses off the picket line. This led to almost all the other horses breaking loose and stampeding through the town and back to the post, right past regimental headquarters and up the hill to the stables.

The repercussions of this little episode can well be imagined, the least of which were that several non-coms lost their stripes. It was the last of the hi-jinks reminiscent of National Guard days, and from then on the troopers took their military duties more seriously. They were made to realize that they were in an army preparing for war and that their playful college fraternity days were over.

But whether they were Squadron A or Squadron C (or Troop B, for that matter), the horsed elements of the regiment took an overweening pride in their spurs and campaign hats (the mechanized troopers wore overseas caps) and looked down from unbelievable heights on their gasoline-powered brethren. They paid for the cockiness, however, for a horse soldier's day was a long and hard one.

The stables were about 500 yards behind the barracks and up a long, sloping hill. Like the barracks they were newly built and smelled of fresh pine, even after they became home to several hundred horses. That's because they were kept spotlessly clean and the slight horsey odor mixing with the pine was a pleasant one (at least to a horse soldier) and never overpowering. The cleaning detail, armed with pitchforks and wheelbarrows, was called "stable police" and was regularly shared by every private and private first class on a rotating basis.

Unlike the barracks, the stables were completed and ready for the regiment when it arrived, and the horses were moved in without discomfort or epidemic. In the old army tradition of R.H.IP. (Rank Has Its Privileges) the troopers' mounts were put into straight stalls, while the few roomy box stalls were reserved for the officers' chargers.

Incidentally, at the time of federalization, each officer had been given the opportunity of buying his own fine mount for just one dollar from the private farms maintained by Squadron A at New City in upstate New York and Squadron C at Huntington, Long Island. Just about every officer took the plunge.

The daily stable police detail took care of feeding the horses and cleaning the stalls, but the entire available troop had to turn out for "water call." Each day, once early in the morning and once again late in the afternoon, the troops marched up the hill to the stables. Each horse was taken out of its stall and led to the concrete watering troughs in the adjoining paddocks to drink its fill. Only after these rituals were completed were the men fed and allowed some leisure.

Leisure, however, was a relative term. Rifles, pistols and machine guns had to be cleaned after the day's exercises, boots polished and spurs shined. And, of course, there were always the inevitable details and fatigues—kitchen police, guard duty, general barracks and latrine cleaning and any number of other chores of the kind that plague a soldier's life. To the New Yorkers of Squadron A the good old armory days of polo and parties as well as the occasional spree at Manhattan nightclubs like the Stork or El Morocco, soon became just a rapidly fading memory.

The weeks stretched into months and the training went on and on. The mechanized troops practiced their road marches, motor vehicle maintenance and radio techniques, and both horse and mechanized units spent time on dismounted squad and platoon tactics as well as the boring close order drill. There was also considerable work on the firing range until almost everyone in the regiment sported some sort of marksmanship badge, from the introductory "Marksman" to the coveted "Expert."

Medical services were efficient, but the newly inducted medical officers were sometimes not totally military in appearance or manner. One veterinary officer became known for returning the troopers' smart cavalry salutes with a wave of his cigar! Nevertheless, most minor ailments were treated and cured at morning sick call, and comparatively few troopers ended up in the hospital.

Those that did, usually the result of an accident with horse or machine, received excellent treatment in the modern, well-equipped post hospital. They also received an enlightening education in how the "other half," the regular army, lived, for in much of the time of the squadron's stay at Devens the post was shared with the 1st Infantry division, the soon to be famous "Big Red One." In these pre-Pearl Harbor days this was still a regular army outfit of tough, efficient "men with the bark on." At hospital mess tables a 101st trooper might be bemused at a regular's loud growl of "salt down!" instead of the more polite request for condiments heard in the mess of his own outfit. He would be fascinated by the perhaps apocryphal tales of savage barroom brawls and stores of the nefarious, but profitable, activity of "rolling" drunks. And, if he were foolish enough to lend a fellow soldier "a few dollars until payday," he would be angered that he never saw the man again. It was an interesting view of another world, but the hospitalized trooper was glad to leave the regulars and return to the comparative gentility of his own regiment.

For after-hours entertainment on the post at Fort Devens there was not a great deal of choice. The most convenient amusement was a visit to the troop "day room" for a game of table tennis, or a trip to the post theater to see a movie. And there was always the possibility of a poker session in the barracks until taps, or a crap game in the latrine after lights out.

A weekend pass might find you on a train to Boston where the preferred rendezvous for Squadron A was the bar at the Ritz, or the Fox and Hounds Lounge on Beacon Street. For a less toney atmosphere, the numerous bars on Washington Street catered to uniformed patrons but were inclined to become somewhat raucous as the hour grew late. Or, if you were lucky, you might meet a local girl and find yourself a home away from home. Some troopers even found wives!

Eventually the troopers were entitled to longer furloughs, making it possible to take the train back to New York to relax for a few days and bask in the adulation their uniforms often brought them. Too soon, however, they found themselves meeting their squadron friends under the clock at the Biltmore, and were back on the train to Fort Devens and the routine of army life.

In August 1941 that routine was relieved by a weeklong maneuver, with the regulars of the 1st Division providing the "enemy." It took place off the reservation and the local townspeople were astonished at the violent display of military activity. The squadron's scout cars and motorcycles dashed back and forth on the roads and horses galloped over the fields and through the woods as the troopers learned a little more about what their duties would be in a real war. It was excellent preparation for the big First Army maneuvers that were scheduled for the following month.

So it was that in September the 101st Cavalry left Fort Devens on its first really long road march as a horse-mechanized regiment, bound for the Carolinas and those important maneuvers that would test the combat readiness of an entire army. The march brought out every vehicle in the regiment, scout cars, motorcycles and trucks as well as the huge portée vans, each of the latter packed with eight horses and eight men and all their equipment.

In due course, after remarkably few breakdowns and other misadventures, this traveling circus arrived at its assigned bivouac area, extensive fields adjacent to the peach orchards near a little town called Candor, in North Carolina. Candor had a few small red brick warehouse type buildings, a barbershop and a little lunchroom with a pretty blonde waitress and a very limited menu. That seemed to be all there was to it. To most of the New Yorkers of the 101st, whose only previous impressions of the southland were caught while passing through on the way to Palm Beach, Lauderdale or Miami, it was a depressing sight. Knowing that Candor would be their base of operations for the better part of the next three months was not a pleasant thought.

However, the troopers didn't have time to dwell on such a gloomy prospect. The very first chore was the creation of picket lines for the horses and motor parks for the vehicles, followed by the pitching of pyramidal tents as sleeping quarters for the men, setting up troop kitchens, digging latrines, providing tables, chairs, typewriters and all the other necessities for processing the paperwork inevitable even in such a mobile unit as a regiment of cavalry.

The next few days were settling-in time. The 2nd Squadron tuned up its vehicles, which had suffered a fair amount of wear and tear on the long trip down. The 1st Squadron exercised its horses on the dirt roads that criss-crossed the area. Because so many men were engaged in finishing the set-up of what was to become a semi-permanent encampment, there was a shortage of exercise riders and most of the troopers ended up riding one and leading one (which was what those in the machine gun platoon normally did anyway).

A real difficulty, however, came at water call. The watering point was along a stream a good distance from the picket line and could be reached only by a narrow, muddy trail. Even without saddles or bridles riding was better than walking, so it was ride one and lead one again, guiding the horses by leg, weight and halter shank. At the watering point itself there was considerable confusion. The banks of the stream were steep, muddy and slippery and the thirsty horses were not always easy to control. Officers directing traffic and attempting to bring some order into the confusion slipped and slid in the mud and sometimes stood ankle deep in the stream, which was not very good for their beautiful custom-made Peal or Dehner riding boots. Somehow or other they were able to straighten things out and in due course water call at base camp became a quiet, orderly, routine affair.

The actual maneuvers began, the 101st Cavalry, horse and machine, found itself in the thick of the action. Not since World War I had any of the New Yorkers seen such a conglomeration of soldiery in one place. There were divisions of infantry, battalions of artillery and more tanks than could be imagined.

There were also swarms of newspaper reporters, for the maneuvers were of nationwide interest. The reporters loved the horses; cavalry was a bit of an oddity in modern warfare, so the 1st Squadron received more than its share of publicity.

A newspaper reporter was interviewing trooper Don Adams, who was wearing fatigues while he was cleaning the stables. The reporter asked him what he did in civilian life. Don replied that he was vice-president of a large bank, but that he was prouder of being a private in Squadron A.

To the newsreel cameramen a cavalry charge was the *pièce de résistance*, and the 101st acceded to their demands and staged one for them, even though this type of maneuver was considered antiquated and had only been practiced by the New York troopers on rare occasions. That made no difference to the cameramen; the charge was a command performance.

Veterans later recalled the occasion. They remember their hearts beating faster as the order was given and the horses formed into a line and moved out at a walk. The next command was "Raise pistol!" followed by "Trot!" then "Gallop!" and, finally, "*Charge!*" A mass of galloping horses thundered across the field, their riders with pistols thrust out before them, right past the cameramen, red and white guidons flapping out in front. The newsreel people got a great shot, one worthy of being shown in theaters nationwide.

Fortunately, the charging line held until the troops were well past the cameras and the order was given to rally. The galloping horses were now thoroughly excited and racing against each other, the riders had dropped their pistols (still hanging from their lanyards and bouncing around) and were using both hands to try to control their mounts. The line had disintegrated into a wild melee and a few horsemen had even ploughed off into the surrounding woods. But after a few very wild moments order was restored, the horses quieted down, pistols returned to their holsters and the re-formed column trotted back past the cameramen who, busy with their work, were unaware of the near debacle that had occurred just beyond their range of vision. Too bad; it would have made an even more exciting picture than the charge itself.

The rest of the maneuvers were less exciting for the cavalrymen, but more valuable as training exercises. The officers learned much about tactics and communications, and polished their leadership skills under difficult conditions. Each man learned the true meaning of his individual MOS (Military Occupational Specialty) whether it was driver, radioman, horse shoer, just plain rifleman or whatever. And all were learning to put up with the hardships of living in the field for long periods of time.

Not that there weren't opportunities for recreation, such as it was, occasional free periods when the lunchroom in Candor was crowded with the New York cavalrymen. Then too, the regiment's reputation had spread to one of the larger nearby communities which arranged for the local girls' college to put on a dance exclusively for the 101st.

The invitation was accepted enthusiastically, but there was a certain amount of disappointment when it was discovered how thoroughly the festivities were to be chaperoned by eagle-eyed Catholic nuns.

And no doubt, when time permitted, some Squadron A men with the right connections were able to take advantage of such well known local watering holes as Pinehurst or Southern Pines, where they might even get in a few rounds of golf or tennis. But for the nature lovers, the many bivouacs deep in the Carolina woods were a kind of vacation in themselves. The lofty pines gave shelter from the southern sun and the thick pine needles provided a soft bed after a hard day's soldiering. And many horse soldiers remembered the occasions when the 1st Squadron forded the mist-shrouded Pee Dee River in the early hours of the morning. This post dawn exercises reminded the troopers of a Hollywood western—every many a John Wayne—as they splashed their horses across the wide and quickening stream. And rumor had it that due to dam construction upstream, the Pee Dee could become a raging torrent at any moment and sweep them all away. It was a prediction that added another touch of theatricality to the scene.

Most of the time, however, the maneuvers were just plain hard work. The climate didn't help. The Carolinas offered blistering heat in the summer and early fall, with accompanying dust on the dry days and mud-slicked misery when it rained. Then, as winter approached and the southland was not so sunny, the biting cold became the greatest source of discomfort, particularly at pre-dawn reveille in the woods. By the beginning of December when the maneuvers ended, the 101st Cavalry was more than ready to come home.

The trip back to Devens was not too pleasant. The cold made riding a motorcycle sheer misery, and it was almost as bad for those in the open scout cars and atop the horse vans. And Troop C suffered a tragic accident when a trooper somehow fell from one of those vans as it barreled along, and was killed. It happened on December 6, 1941, on the eve of Pearl Harbor, so it might almost be said that Pfc. Bobby Block was the 101st Cavalry's first casualty of World War II.

Different elements of the regiment arrived back at Fort Devens at different times and some were already there on that historic December 7. But there are horse troopers who recall bivouacking at the United States Military Academy at West Point on December 6, all unaware of what fate had in store for them. Their horse vans pulled onto the parade grounds at the academy in mid-afternoon as groups of cadets and their officer-instructors watched. Among the onlookers was Major General Robert Eichelberger, the academy's superintendent, mounted on a beautiful thoroughbred. He was later to gain fame as commander of the U.S. Eighth Army in the Pacific.

The spit-and-polish cadets must have been shocked by the appearance of the cavalrymen after almost three months in the field and several days on the road. Dusty, torn, unkempt, just plain dirty, was an accurate description. To add to the unmilitary appearance, the preferred headgear was the ugly "cap, winter," and several of the troopers had souvenir Dixieland coonskin tails dangling from the back of their caps, *a la* Daniel Boone. But in spite of their looks there was a swagger to the booted and spurred New Yorkers—as well as a distinct odor of horse.

The men picketed their horses inside the academy's huge riding hall and that night slept on the tanbark floor beside them. Being under a roof was sheer luxury after so long beneath canvas or sky, and to the troopers the indoor ring was comparable to the finest luxury hotel.

The following morning the convoy loaded up and pulled out of West Point for the last leg of the journey back to Devens. The date was December 7, 1941. Gradually the troopers noticed that people in the towns the convoy passed through seemed more animated and interested in the soldiers than usual—and some of them were even cheering! Soon the reason became obvious as the passers-by called out the news. Pearl Harbor had been bombed!

Surprisingly, the men took the news calmly, even joked about it, although they knew the promise of the regiment being released from federal service and back in New York in the next few weeks would be broken and their own dreams shattered. Instead of griping, however, there was an air of grim determination as the convoy pulled into Devens and the men settled down to the serious business of war.

The next few weeks saw a flurry of excitement and hectic activity at the fort. Details from the 101st were sent to guard the airfield at Bangor, Maine, where combat planes were being ferried across the Atlantic to join the British. Guard duty on the remote runways of Dow Air Base was a cold and lonely job in the snowy Maine winter but the troopers always managed to find some free time, and later told wild tales of the bars and nightclubs of Bangor.

There were also details from the 101st assigned to guard trains loaded with airplane parts and other emergency military equipment on the long stop-and-go journey out to the west coast, where a Japanese attack was momentarily expected. But this duty appeared to be all work and no play, and the stories told by the returning troopers were not as amusing as those of the Maine veterans. And, of course, for those not engaged in these extra activities there was the usual endless training, although this time more intensified than ever.

In the midst of all this brouhaha the 1st Squadron was inundated with a draft of new horses, fresh from the remount depot at Front Royal, Virginia. This was the second group of remounts to joint the regiment, the first having been trained sometime prior to the Carolina maneuvers. This time, however, because of the war the allotted training time was only two months instead of the usual three. To do the job, another remount detail was hastily assembled, for which there were plenty of volunteers.

As was usual in the 101st Cavalry, the training group was a potpourri of Squadron A. Squadron C and upstate troopers, commanded by upstate Lieutenant William Wadsworth, who later became known in horsey circles as master of the Geneseo Hunt and president of the national Master of Foxhounds Association. The NCO who directed the training was Sergeant Bill Stefurak of Squadron C, who was considered one of the unit's top horsemen and who became a member of Squadron A after the war.

Army regulations required that before horses could be turned over to the regiments they had to be ridden by the men of the remount depots to determine their suitability as cavalry mounts. It turned out, however, that the term "ridden" was a rather loose one. The troopers of the 101st maintained that at least some of the horses they received had been ridden for just a few seconds before they had bucked off their remount depot riders—and were then sent along to the regiment.

When the new horses arrived they were assigned to their riders by lot. Every army horse had an identification number imprinted on his neck, the so-called Preston brand. These numbers were put into a hat and each trooper drew two numbers. They were his horses for the duration of the training period and whether they were quiet, soft-gaited treasures or wild, bucking devils, he was stuck with them.

These new horses were a peculiar assortment. While many developed into good troop horses, others were quite unsuitable. There were some ultra-excitable thoroughbreds, a few strangely-paced saddle breds, some draft types and more than one were overage or lame. The reduced training time made matters even more difficult, but eventually the remounts were more or less trained, the unfit ones weeded out and the rest distributed among the three horse troops.

Hardly had this occurred when disaster struck. The 1st Squadron was mechanized. The order came down as a result of the Carolina maneuvers. The experimental concept of horse-mechanized regiments was an interesting one, but apparently it hadn't worked. The capabilities of the two different elements did not match and they hadn't operated as well together as the army brass had hoped. In addition, the big tractor trailers used to haul the horses were unwieldy, almost impossible to camouflage, difficult to turn around in a limited space and frequently bogged down in mud and took forever to extricate. The horse-mechanized idea was abandoned throughout the army and the dispirited troopers of the 1st Squadron of the 101st Cavalry were condemned to travel around in scout cars and ride motorcycles. Losing their spurs and exchanging those dashing campaign hats with the yellow hat cords for the commonplace overseas caps that everyone else in the army wore was a hard blow indeed.

There was a final, somewhat informal mounted review at Devens before the horses were loaded on the vans for the last, long journey down to the Front Royal remount depot in Virginia and there was hardly a dry eye when the troopers turned their mounts out into the depot's lush pastures. The trip back to Devens was largely a grim and silent one for the ex-horse soldiers.

By the time the convoy reached New England the men had a chance to reflect on the positive aspects of the situation. Without the horses to take care of, the journey home was almost like a vacation. And after a few days back at the post came the realization of how easy mechanized life could be. No more stable police, no more water call. No more lugging a heavy McClellan saddle loaded with bedroll and saddle bags up the hill to the stables on the morning of a field exercise. And no more hours of grooming after a hard day's work. Yes, mechanized life was a picnic compared to the old horse days.

There was plenty for the newly mechanized troopers to learn, however. Besides driving and being introduced to the mysteries of "first echelon" vehicle maintenance, there was radio school where an entirely new class was involved in the *dits* and *dahs* of the Morse code. The radio school was a typical conglomeration of 101st troopers of all three origins; the commander was Lieutenant Halsey Downer of Squadron A, the chief instructor was Sergeant Carlos Bernstein of

Squadron C and there was, as always, a sprinkling of "apple knockers" from upstate Troop B.

Soon the former horsemen of the 1st Squadron were as much "tin can" soldiers as their companions in arms, but there were times when the entire regiment was reminded of its previous status as horse cavalry. One such occasion was the visit of Queen Wilhelmina of the Netherlands to Fort Devens. She represented the Dutch government in exile and reviewed a march past of all the troops on the post. These included the 1st Infantry Division with its splendid band, as well as the entire 101st Cavalry, dismounted but still wearing boots and breeches. As the cavalry marched past the reviewing stand the band struck up "The Old Gray Mare, She Ain't What She Used To Be!" It was a rather snide and painful reminder of the glory days of the horse soldiers and did nothing to foster any kind feelings they might have had toward the "Big Red One."

By this time the regiment was losing some of its best men, many going off to Officer Candidate School or becoming cadre for other units. Since federalization there had been a slow, steady drain of senior non-coms being selected for the 90-day OCS course at the cavalry school at Fort Riley, Kansas. Although it was a general army policy *not* to send recent graduates back to the original units, this did not always hold true in the 101st Cavalry, and some ex-sergeants came back to the regiment as second lieutenants. While this was generally thought of as bad for discipline, it was in accordance with an old Squadron A tradition that "discipline in the squadron is simply a gentlemen's agreement on the part of the enlisted men to accede to the wishes of the officers." In the case of the 101st Cavalry to practice it certainly did no harm, but the longer the Squadron continued in federal service, the further this quaint idea of "gentlemen's agreement" disappeared into the mists of legend, and the hard fact of army discipline emerged.

Other officers' schools claimed many more squadron men, including the infantry school at Fort Benning, Georgia and the anti-aircraft artillery school at Camp Davis, North Carolina. And several officers were simply transferred to the 1st Cavalry Division at Fort Bliss, Texas. Among the latter was that paladin of Squadron A, Major "Tubby" Tuckerman, who ended the war a colonel commanding a regiment of that division in combat in the Philippines–although, alas, it had by then been converted into infantry. (After the war Tubby rose to become a reserve Major General commanding the 77th Division.)

All the while fresh recruits were coming into the 101st to fill the vacancies caused by the losses to officer candidate schools. These replacements were recent draftees, totally green as far as military training was concerned, and the regiment found itself in the same condition as Squadron A had been when it became the 105th Machine Gun Battalion in World War I.

Once again quoting from Colonel Graydon, "Soon the regiment became a truly cosmopolitan outfit with New Yorkers, farmers, hillbillies, cowboys, mill workers, Indians and many other types." Temporary units were established, staffed by regimental officers and NCO's to put the new men through basic training. During this period the regular troops could sometimes assemble less than thirty men at drill call. Under these conditions there was little chance of the regiment being called for overseas service. However, the regiment was proud of the fact that it had a higher percentage of NCOs going to OCS than perhaps any other unit in the army.

Before we go on to further activities of the 101st Cavalry, mention should be made of a strange and eerie happening within the regiment. It was rumored that there had been an attack upon a sentry, even a murder, at night in the area of the now deserted stables. Like most rumors, the story was vague, at least as it came down to the troops. At that time the 45th Division, a National Guard unit from Oklahoma, was also stationed at Fort Devens. Since it contained many Indians (its divisional insignia was the mystical thunderbird, in Indian mythology the personification of thunder and lightning in a huge bird), the attack incident came to be thought of as part of an Indian ritual and the victim was said to have been bound in a specifically Indian manner.

True or not, the regimental brass took the matter seriously, so much so that special orders were given to the stable sentries. Hereafter (or at least for the next few weeks) the interior guard in the stable area was to patrol in pairs—in addition to their pistols were issued shotguns, a more serious close-in weapon than rifle. That much is known to be fact.

There were no more incidents, but the troopers reported a distinctly unpleasant feeling on nocturnal patrol in the deserted stables. Nor did the word ever come down de-mystifying the situation. Nobody ever seemed to know what actually happened, what really occurred to start the rumors and motivate the precautions taken to safeguard the sentries.

Less threatening but almost as bizarre as the sentry incident was the live falcon that showed up in a cage in regimental headquarters. It was apparently a publicity stunt for the then current film, "The Maltese Falcon"–and supposedly as a gift from Humphrey Bogart himself. The connection to the regiment, albeit tenuous, was the falcon, "close and belled," on the regimental insignia.

In September 1942, the regiment was ordered to Pine Camp (its old National Guard summer encampment in upstate New York) for eight more weeks of intensive field training. After that it was back to Devens–for the last time. No more would the men of the 101st Cavalry stand reveille at dawn and retreat at dusk on the snowy troop streets during a fierce New England winter. They now had their orders to head for Maryland and an entirely new assignment.

CHAPTER 3. AT LAST – COMBAT!

THE new home station of the 101st Cavalry was now Fort Meade, Maryland, where it became the mobile reserve of the Eastern Defense Command. Its job was to patrol the coastal regions from Maryland to South Carolina, to defend it from spies or saboteurs who might be landed by parachute or submarine. It was a difficult yet boring assignment, and officers and men were becoming impatient. They had been in federal service more than two years now and the war in Europe was reaching its climax. It was time to get into the fighting.

The regiment, however, was to endure yet more training before it received orders for overseas duty. In the summer of 1943 Colonel Gilbert Ackerman, who had been the regimental commander since 1938, was replaced by Colonel Charles B. McClelland, a tough, enthusiastic young officer who was eventually to lead it into battle.

But first there was a complete reorganization of the regiment, which was now called the 101st Cavalry Group. Under this headquarters umbrella were two separate mechanized cavalry squadrons, the 101st and 116th. Each had added to it a 75 mm assault gun troop and a light tank company. There would be another interchange of officers, in a move typical of the 101st Cavalry's recent history, Colonel McClelland retained command, with Lieutenant Colonel Leo Mortensen, 101st Cavalry (Squadron C), as his executive officer. The 116th Cavalry Squadron was now commanded by Lieutenant Colonel Hubert "Butch" Leonard, also a Squadron C man, and his executive officer was Henry Brock of Squadron A. And there were many other changes yet to come.

At about this time the group received its new weapons and vehicles, including M8 armored cars, assault guns and light tanks. It had just enough time to train with this unfamiliar equipment, when it was ordered overseas.

In November 1944, the 101st Cavalry Group embarked from the Brooklyn army base, and a few weeks later found itself in England. The passage, on a former luxury liner packed to the brim with soldiers and equipment, had been uncomfortable, like all overseas troop movements. And then, as usual, it was "hurry up and wait," for the 101st did not find itself actually facing the enemy until the end of February 1945.

Two excellent volumes have already been written, giving in full detail the accomplishments of the 101st Cavalry in action in World War II. They are the monograph of Colonel Graydon, *The 101st Cavalry in World War II*, and *Wingfoot–The Official History of the 101st Cavalry Group*, edited by Major Mercer W. Sweeney, published for members of the group and printed in Germany immediately after the war. ("Wingfoot" was the code name of the group during its overseas service.)

We have included Colonel Graydon's work in our appendix, and now continue with just the highlights of the two campaigns, Rhineland and Central Europe, in which the 101st took part.

As February drew to a close, the 101st was moved up to replace the 106th Cavalry, which had been in defensive positions along the French-German border in the U.S. Seventh Army area. The advance of the entire American army had been held up by supply problems, complicated by the German offensive in the Ardennes, known as the Battle of the Bulge. Now that this situation was cleared up, the Allied Forces, from the North Sea to the Swiss border, were prepared for the final battles of the war. And the men of the 101st were about to receive their baptism under fire.

They were ready. The years of preparation, training and reorganization in the States had not been wasted. The men were physically tough, mentally awake and thoroughly prepared for the job ahead. Moreover, they were now reinforced by the attachment of units of field artillery, engineers and 4.2 inch mortar battalion. In addition, there were smaller units that were now part of the group, including an air support party, a prisoner interrogation team, a military government detachment and a counter intelligence detachment. It was, indeed, a small army, and it was all under command of the 101st Cavalry Group.

For the next 85 days the 101st was almost continually in combat. The fighting was fierce, the Germans were fighting on their own soil and had put into effect all the defensive tactics they had learned since North Africa and nearly two years of slow, stubborn retreat. Here, in their first contact with the enemy along the Saar River front, the men of the 101st encountered the horror of mines, booby traps and

SQUADRON A HIGH ROLLERS TAKE OVER THE DINING CAR FOR A LITTLE FRIENDLY AFTER-HOURS CARD GAME ON THE WAY TO PINE CAMP.

LIEUTENANT COLONEL EDMUND BELLINGER, (LEFT) COMMANDING OFFICER OF THE MANHATTAN UNITS, 51ST INFANTRY NYG (SQUADRON A), CONFERS WITH LIEUTENANT ROBERT WILSON. THE SCENE IS CAMP SMITH, PEEKSKILL, N.Y., WORLD WAR II.

TROOPER WITH SQUADRON A HORSES

shellfire. In early March the order was given to attack and all units of the 101st plunged into their initial offensive action.

A particularly tough nut to crack was a strong enemy position on Hill 283 that dominated the battlefield, but Troop A of the 101st Squadron, taking heavy casualties, finally captured the hill. All the other troops of the 101st, operating separately, did equally well. Some, sweeping down the roads in their armored cars, mopped up the little towns that dotted the west bank of the Saar River. Others, fighting on foot, performed like veterans against the best the Germans had to offer. The price was 33 casualties; dead, wounded and missing.

Week after week the fighting continued with little letup. The Germans were now in full retreat, leaving pockets of resistance behind. Sometimes these surrendered promptly, and sometimes there was no resistance at all. But more often the defenders fought as stubbornly and as fiercely as at any time during the war. They used machine guns, mortars and artillery, including the dreaded 88s and the deadly Nebelwerfers, the "screaming meemies" rocket projectors so feared by the Allied troops. And barbed wire, mines and the ever-present booby traps added to the horror.

As the 101st passed through the Siegfried Line, crossed the Rhine and pierced deeper into Germany, signs of German breakdown became more obvious, particularly among the civilians, who were happy to see Americans rather than Russians. At the same time, the pockets of resistance and the German counter attacks became fiercer, especially when the Americans met up with units of fanatical SS troops.

A case in point is the attack by 101st Group troopers on the little town of Merkendorf, where they ran into remnants of the 17th SS Panzer Division. The Germans, after being driven back, counter attacked. The fighting degenerated into that trickiest of combat, house-to-house and hand-to-hand. Captain Lou Bossert, who had been federalized with the 101st as a sergeant, gone to OCS and returned to the regiment as a second lieutenant and was now commanding officer of Troop C of the 116th Cavalry Squadron, described the situation, "The troop command post was attacked by panzer faust (rocket) fire and four SS troopers were killed as they attempted to enter the windows. For over two hours a series of bloody hand-to-hand battles were fought throughout the town. Attackers were repelled by small arms, knives and furniture thrown from the windows."

When the fighting was over the cavalry was in possession of the town. Eighty SS troopers had been killed, 16 captured and an undetermined number wounded. The Americans had suffered only 19 casualties.

Another outstanding operation was that of "Task Force Brock," led by Major Henry Brock of Squadron A. When the 101st Reconnaissance Squadron was unable to penetrate the defenses of Wildenstein, the squadron commander, Lieutenant Colonel Milton Kendall, ordered Major Brock, who was now his executive officer, to organize a task force to get the job done. Brock formed his force from B Troop of the 101st Squadron and B Troop of the 116th, the latter drawn from the group reserve. Troop C of the 101st had already slipped around behind the German force and was ready to attack it from the rear. Major Brock gave the order, and all three troops attacked from both directions. The battle lasted a good three hours and when the smoke cleared the resistance had been broken and Wildenstein was in the hands of the 101st.

There was never any clear cut pattern for the operations of the 101st Cavalry Group in the pursuit of a not quite beaten German army across Germany. As the group continued east, sometimes some units acted in the traditional cavalry role of scouting and patrolling while others fought pitched battles with the enemy. Often the cavalry was accompanied by attached field artillery or medium tanks whose heavier guns blasted out enemy strongholds that had stopped the lightly armed cavalry. And sometimes the 101st was attacked from the air, increasingly by the newly deployed jet planes of the Luftwaffe.

The advance of the 101st Cavalry was bitterly opposed until very nearly the end, when it raced down the autobahn and turned south into the Alps. Then, in early May, the group received the message that the Germans had surrendered. The fighting was over for the men of the 101st.

For a more detailed account of the group's adventures in Europe see the appendix of this volume. Here you will find Colonel Graydon's monograph, the day-to-day story, told in a precise, accurate military manner, yet with compassion and humor, by someone who was there all the way, from pre-war National Guard days in New York to the de-activating the wartime 101st in November 1945.

The western European odyssey of the 101st Cavalry was not the only World War II scene for the men of Squadron A. As we have seen, many men who started their military careers with the squadron ended the war in responsible positions all over the world, from infantry combat in the steaming jungles of Burma to anti-aircraft artillery watch in the frigid ports of Iceland–and even on the high seas.

While it would be impossible to recount the adventures of every squadron veteran of World War II, a few outstanding examples might point out the variety of their service. Perhaps the most celebrated of these soldiers was Alfred G. "Tubby" Tuckerman, who enlisted in Squadron A in 1927, was a major commanding the horse squadron at Fort Devens for a year, and then joined the 1st Cavalry Division at Fort Bliss, Texas, where he was operations officer (S-3) of the 12th Cavalry. When the division was ordered overseas in 1943, he commanded the advance detachment of 3,000 men and subsequently laid out and built the division camp and training area outside of Brisbane, Australia. In combat he progressed from operations officer of a regiment to operations officer of the division (G-3) and eventually to operations officer of I Corps, where he was one of the planners of the Lingayen Gulf landings in the Philippines. He was back in the 1st Cavalry Division as a brigade executive officer when it first entered Manila, and he was in command of the 8th Cavalry Regiment during the landing at Yokohama and the occupation of Japan. Among the decorations Tubby was proud to wear were the Silver Star, the Legion of Merit, the Bronze Star with two Oak Leaf Clusters and the Air Medal.

While such tried and true Squadron A men as Colonel Bill Roberson, who was on the staff of the First Army in Europe, could be said to be working on the same level as Colonel Tuckerman, there was one who occupied an even more rarified position in the conflict. That was Henry L. Stimson, a sergeant in Squadron A in the Spanish American War, who was actually Secretary of War throughout World War II!

Coming down from Olympus, we can cite a few month (among the very many) squadron men who served in so many far flung parts of the world. CBI, the China-India-Burma Theater, seems to be an area that absorbed many. Bill Rand, one of the Squadron's top polo players both before and after the war, was a lieutenant colonel commanding a remount depot in India. His outfit supplied hundreds of the mules that made operations in the rugged terrain of that part of the world possible for such Squadron men as Bill Dunham, Clary Jochum and Bill Shepard.

Captain Bill Dunham, also serving in CBI, perhaps deserves special mention for his quick thinking when his Chinese troops were stalled by what looked like and impossible river crossing. Early monsoons had turned the Salween River into a raging flood, and many men were drowned when their rubber boats overturned. Bill's commanding officer was about to give up and order a retreat, but Bill had a better idea. His men used the cables from the winches on the trucks to improvise a "breeches buoy" operation from the top of the cliffs. The troops rode across in the rubber boats suspended from the winch cables, which prevented them from being swept away. They established a bridgehead on the far side and went on to win the campaign.

Overhead, Bucko McCoun, now in the Air Force, was "flying the Hump" over the Himalayas in the dangerous supply run between Indian and China, while Larry Larkin and Herb Martin had left Fort Devens to become liaison officers to the Chinese army.

Wyllis Terry had also departed the 101st at Devens to join the 1st Cavalry Division at Fort Bliss and in the Pacific Theatre, and ex-trooper J. L. Cooper served in Italy with VI Corps, Robert Carlson with a tank destroyer battalion in Central Europe, Frank Lane with an engineer outfit in France and H. Harding Isaacson with a heavy bombardment group in the Air Force. Ed Allen, with the 1st Cavalry Division in the occupation of Japan, used his equestrian experience to discover an excellent riding horse for himself–that turned out to have been the parade horse of Crown Prince Akihito, who was later Emperor. (Nothing but the best for Squadron A!) Of course, Halsey Downer and Henry Brock stayed with the 101st cavalry until the triumphant end in Germany.

The squadron was well represented on the high seas, too. Herb Raff, who had joined F Troop in 1936, and who was President and then Chairman of the Squadron A Association, served for three and a half years in the South Pacific on the aircraft carrier *Yorktown*, and was on the shakedown cruise of the *Intrepid*. Otto Kinzel, later president of the Association, was also a wartime Navy man, serving on the battleship *Iowa*.

When the smoke of World War II had cleared, 44 members of Squadron A had been killed in action or had died in the service. Squadron A people had been awarded two Medals of Honor, 32 Croix de Guerre, five French Legion of Honor awards, five Orders of the British Empire and ten Distinguished Flying Crosses, plus a number of Silver Stars, Bronze Stars and Air Medals. It was, to say the least, quite a record.

HERBERT K. RAFF, PRESIDENT 1981-85, CHAIRMAN 1985-1990. RAFF WAS AN OFFICER ON THE AIRCRAFT CARRIER *U.S.S. YORKTOWN* DURING WORLD WAR II.

CHAPTER 4. HOME FROM THE WARS

EVEN before the squadron was actually called into federal service it was known that a unit would be needed to replace it at home. As early as 1940 there was an authorization from New York to organize a "State Guard" battalion to fill in for the federalized National Guard troops and occupy the armory when the time came, just as the "Depot Troop" did when the squadron was called up in World War I. But preparations were under way long before the official word came down.

In October the Ex-Members Association notified all former members of Squadron A that a new State Guard regiment, the 51st Infantry, was being formed and the Manhattan units of this outfit would be the successors to Squadron A. According to Lieutenant Colonel Bill Brookfield, a former Squadron A member and one of the organizers of the new battalion, within a month the ranks of the Manhattan units of the 51st Infantry Regiment were filled and had a waiting list.

The new men were of all ages. The "older" volunteers were usually ex-members of Squadron A and their friends, doing their patriotic duty. Among the younger men were those ineligible for the draft because of some minor physical disability, or who held civilian positions vital to the war effort. More often they were simply men awaiting their draft call and getting valuable military training while doing so. But whatever their origins they were patriots all, and by the end of the war it is estimated that some 50 percent or more of the men of the 51st Infantry ended up in the national armed forces, a great many as officers.

It took a while for this new Squadron A to receive its equipment, and at first the men drilled in the armory in civilian clothes and without arms. Eventually they received uniforms; U.S. Army fatigues, leggings, shoes and overseas caps, and they were armed with M1917 Enfield rifles of World War I vintage. But what they lacked in the latest weaponry and equipment they made up in enthusiasm, and were soon a well-disciplined, efficient body. Recruiting during the war years was not a problem, for when one of the younger men in the state guard was called to the colors the next man on the waiting list replaced him.

The 51st Infantry easily slipped into the routine that had so long been that of Squadron A, with drill night once a week and two weeks summer camp, this time at Camp Smith, the state military reservation at Peekskill, N.Y. In addition to the summer encampment there was also scheduled weekend rifle practice on the range at Smith, where the 51st acquitted itself well.

When the war ended the work of the state guard continued on and it would be many months before the National Guard would again be organized to replace the state-sponsored units. In the 51st training continued apace and a new interest in horses would arise. During the war a few of the old mounts, not quite fit for active military service, had been kept at the armory and were used for recreational purposes. (One of these, a mare named "Queen of Hearts," was remembered by old timers as a famous squadron polo pony—and she still had many active years as a pleasure horse ahead of her.) And now the post-war U.S. Army, totally mechanized, was offering its surplus cavalry horses for sale at bargain price and Squadron A snapped up a few prime head. A few more very useful mounts were acquired from various sources and donated to the squadron by ex-members. At the armory it began to look like old times again.

Encouraged by the commander of the Manhattan units of the 51st, Major E. "Laddie" Bellinger, the horse activities increased. Major Bellinger was a West Pointer and a former squadron member who had brought the state guard unit to a peak of perfection and who realized the recruiting and public relations value of having the horses in the armory. Now many old squadron people, mustered out of the army, began filtering back into the guard and the 51st profited by their experience.

Not all of these were actually ex-members; some were relatives of members and others had various connections, but all had impressive war records. Among the first veterans to join was Jerome R.A. Monks, whose brother had been a squadron member in the thirties. Jerry was very soon a company commander. He had graduated from infantry OCS at Fort Benning during the war and served with the hard-fighting 34th Infantry Division in North Africa and Italy. Among his many medals was the Distinguished Service Cross, the second highest decoration for valor in the U.S. Army. His colorful tales of wartime action were as inspiring to his guardsmen, young and old, as was his practical military instruction.

Also among the returning veterans was a quiet, unassuming trooper named Harry Disston who joined the 51st soon after the war ended and was appointed sergeant. The only signs that might lead you to guess that he had been a colonel in the Pacific theatre during the war was his chest full of ribbons and the 1st Cavalry Division patch on his right shoulder. Harry was also a well-known horseman and author on equestrian subjects, and it was the rebirth of horse activities that had attracted him to the squadron. Many months later when the National Guard was reconstituted, he left the squadron to become commanding officer of the 107th Infantry, the famous Seventh Regiment, but returned often to ride and referee the polo games. His son, Robin, later became a member of the active squadron.

Another World War II veteran attracted by the horse activities was J. Dudley Lewis, a pre-war Seventh Regiment man, whose wartime experience was a rather unique one; he was a captain attached as supervisory officer to the Chinese field artillery in Burma. Since Dud's unit had American 75mm howitzers packed on mules, and no motor transport, he rode a horse throughout the war. When the Squadron became National Guard again, Captain Lewis served on the staff (ironically, as motor officer).

At about this time the National Horse Show at Madison Square Garden was revived after a wartime hiatus and Squadron A was asked to once again serve as escort to the military teams in the traditional parade on opening night. The Squadron accepted, but it was not so easy to organize. First, there were not yet enough horses in the armory to provide a full escort. That problem was solved by John Burns, a member who was also a professional horseman. During the war John had been a Coast Guardsman, patrolling the Atlantic beaches on horseback, guarding against spies and saboteurs who might possibly have been landed by submarine. Now he and his brother operated a riding academy on the west side, one of the largest in Manhattan, and generously loaned enough horses to the Squadron to make up the shortage.

The next problem was uniforms. Enough old hussar tunics and busbies were dug out of squadron storerooms to do the job—almost. The big hitch was size. The uniforms had originally been tailored for another generation and World War II's group were a bit larger. Some trading around among the members of the escort provided a more or less satisfactory solution, although a few of the bigger men were never entirely comfortable.

Another problem—there were no breeches available, but this one was ingeniously solved when each man was asked to contribute his own black tuxedo trousers. These, with a yellow strip sewn temporarily down the side, and black shoes, blended beautifully with the sky blue tunics. Led by Major Walter B. Devereux, the New York Hussars were ready to ride again!

The movement of the escort from the armory through Central Park and down Eighth Avenue to the Garden was uneventful, but the actual entrance into the bright lights and enthusiastic crowd of the arena provided a few unwelcome thrills. The horses, some of them quite green, were more than a little excited by the unfamiliar scene, and the riders, some of them also quite green, had a bit of difficulty controlling them. The drums and cymbals of the excellent (but loud) First Army Band did not help matters at all and the troopers were lucky to get through the ceremonies without any major disaster. In fact, by and large it all went well enough and the squadron was invited back to provide the escort for many years to come, as it had for so many years before.

With the spirit of the horse now so pervasive in the armory, the return of polo was inevitable and a new polo club appeared on the scene. It was managed by a professional, Al Parsells, a hard-hitting colorful figure with one eye and a rating of eight goals. His popularity with the crowd was almost matched by that of his number one pony, a fast, turn-on-a-dime piebald, whose performance under Parsells often made the difference in a tight game. Polo brought back, both as players and spectators, many ex-members who had been off to the wars. Among the players were Walter Devereux, Phil Brady, Walter Phillips, Zenas Colt and Billy Rand. Harry Disston, now colonel of the Seventh, returned to the armory on Saturday nights to referee, alternating in that capacity with Johnny Burns.

Riding classes for members and their guests were now organized, the adults riding one evening a week, while a children's class was held during the day after school. Another group was put together to form a "Horse Troop" that rode in uniform, drilled as cavalry, participated in city-wide parades and actually received recognition from Albany as part of the state guard.

For the more advanced riders there was a one-evening-a-week jumping class under ex-member Charles M. Bernuth, who had enlisted in the squadron in 1931 and served during the war as a riding instructor at the army's cavalry school at Fort Riley, Kansas. Later he was a captain in the O.S.S. (Office of Strategic Services) and parachuted behind the lines in France to help organize the French resistance. When asked why he had chosen to volunteer for such a dangerous mission, Charlie replied, "I was scared to death at the thought of jumping out of an airplane, so I felt that I just had to test myself." It was in that spirit that Charlie contributed so much to the revitalization of horse activities in the Squadron after the war.

Along with the horses, the social whirl returned to the armory. The black-tie Saturday night polo dances were re-introduced, held after the games in that part of the armory known as the "Squad Room." This sizable hall had actually been the riding ring before the reconstruction of the armory in 1925 and was now used as a troop assembly room. After the game each week it was turned into a ballroom where the troopers and their elegantly turned out ladies could dance the night away. A less formal soiree was the bi-weekly Sunday afternoon "Tea Dance," popular with the social lions of the squadron, but where tea was definitely not on the beverage list.

During this period the Ex-members Room was a favorite place to enjoy after-drill refreshment, and its balcony, overlooking the arena, provided an excellent view of the polo games. In addition, another restaurant was created on the ground floor of the armory in a space previously used as offices. Very attractively decorated, this cozy dining room provided a before drill refuge for troopers and a uniquely inviting rendezvous for polo games and other special occasions. The manager, *maitre d'hotel* and culinary genius who kept this place running so smoothly was an ex-member, a well-known restaurateur who provided an excellent menu and wine list–and did so at remarkably reasonable prices, a boon to the younger guardsmen. The speciality of the house was a very dry double martini, known as the "Squadrini."

It must not be thought that in this rebirth of Squadron A's traditional social activity, military duties were neglected. Recruiting continued, weekly drills went on, and the two-week summer encampment at Camp Smith was accomplished with the usual efficiency and enthusiasm. And there was one serious emergency when key personnel were summoned to the armory by telephone. This was the great blizzard of the winter of 1946-47. The snows hit New York City hard and many streets were blocked. City life came to a virtual standstill, yet troopers managed to get to the armory to put skid chains on the trucks and scout cars and stand ready for whatever duty they were called upon to do. It was not to be, however; the city's police, fire and sanitation departments came through, as they so often do, and on that occasion the guard was not needed.

One of the last of the major social events held in the armory during the state guard period was the squadron's 60th Anniversary dinner. The only space in the armory large enough for such a gala occasion was the drill shed itself, and long, linen-covered tables filled the huge arena on that memorable evening. The gathering was an enormous success with virtually the entire squadron attending, and ex-members showed up from everywhere. It was black tie, of course, and the miniature medals worn by so many of the guests celebrated every battlefield of the recent war and lent an added touch of color to the affair.

While squadron officers labored to maintain the efficiency of the state guard units in their charge, their superiors in Albany and Washington were busy with the paperwork needed to re-create a new National Guard unit to replace the state guard in the 94th Street armory. Eventually their efforts came to fruition and the 101st Cavalry Reconnaissance Squadron (Mecz.), so recently mustered out of federal service, was reborn in the latter part of 1947. It was under command of Lieutenant Colonel Montgomery H. Robbins, an ex-member who had served in Squadron A from 1934 to 1937. He took over from Lieutenant Colonel Edgar A. Kniffen who had joined the squadron in 1931 and served in the Army Air Force in the war. Later the mechanized squadron was commanded by Lieutenant Colonel Walter B. Devereux, a Squadron A member since 1934 and a polo star who played the galloping game almost to its last days in the armory. In World War II he served in the OSS.

The new outfit was not much different than any of its other Squadron A predecessors. Like all of those who had gone before, the new command was concerned, first and foremost, with military efficiency. This was assured by the caliber of its officers, mostly old squadron men fresh from battlefields around the world. These were veterans who had held commissions in the wartime Army (and a few in the Navy and Marines), and some gladly took reductions in rank to be part of the squadron again. Lieutenant colonels became captains, captains became lieutenants and the new unit had a splendid cadre of experienced, battle-hardened officers to help get it started. And while the old 51st State Guard regiment was quietly demobilized, many of its men simply transferred to the new National Guard squadron, bringing with them that traditional Squadron A insouciance so often covered up a very real feeling of military pride and patriotism.

There were problems, of course. The big difference from the good old days was that instead of dealing with horses and sabers, the troopers were now involved with tanks and half-tracks, which called for a whole new training effort. The returning officers themselves had been commissioned in a variety of arms and services and many now required waivers to perform the duties inherent in mechanized cavalry. For the next few years almost all officers were burning the midnight oil, studying the particular techniques of armored warfare offered by army mail order extension courses, and classes in the armory.

New equipment poured in, including jeeps, command cars, light tanks and half-tracks, and Squadron A troopers learned to use them all. Tanks rumbled over the tanbark of the drill shed until horrified state engineers discovered that the arena floor could not take the strain and might collapse momentarily with too much tank activity. After that a few armored vehicles were relegated to the basement and used for armory training, while most were stored at Camp Smith and brought out only for the occasional weekends and for the summer exercises at Camp Drum.

The summer encampments themselves changed considerably. The new location was Camp Drum in Plattsburg, New York, up near the Canadian border in the area where the 1939 maneuvers had been held. It was now a permanent U.S. Army installation and things were more military than in the old days. But so was the National Guard, and the Squadron A units received high marks for their performance.

Along with all the new equipment the squadron had also received a new regular army instructor, Lieutenant Colonel Donald W. Thackeray. "Thack" was perfect for Squadron A. A West Pointer, he was a pre-war horse cavalryman (11th Cavalry, presidio of Monterey, California) whose later wartime assignments had been as an intelligence officer in England, France, Germany, Russia and Austria and with the 5th Infantry Division in Patton's Third Army. He not only kept the squadron on its military toes, but took an active part in its horse activities as well. Besides refereeing Saturday night polo, he coached an embryo horse show team of surplus army horses and ex- and active troopers and whipped it into shape for the local schooling shows that were held periodically in the armory. He also arranged for squadron riders to fox hunt with the Oaks Hunt on Long Island, and members of the hunt were, in turn, loyal supporters of the armory shows.

Besides the schooling shows the squadron also reintroduced the popular spring Horse Show that drew the best horses and riders from all over the east and was considered second only to the National Horse Show at Madison Square Garden as the most important indoor show in the country. As for the National itself, the squadron had a close relationship with it from its earliest days. The troopers of the squadron not only supplied escorts for the international teams in the opening ceremonies, but also supplied two of its latter day presidents, Major General Alfred G. Tuckerman and Lieutenant Colonel Walter B. Devereux. And there were always a number of squadron men on the show's various committees.

In the years after World War II the squadron also offered stabling and training space for the international teams a week or so before the Madison Square Garden show opened. Observing the best horsemen from all over the world as they worked their beautifully schooled horses over the jumps in the armory provided fascinating and instructive entertainment for many of the squadron's admiring horse enthusiasts.

The stars of the international teams of the late forties and fifties were the Mexicans (they were the winners of the 1948 Olympics in London–and just about every possible award at the National) and since they were the only team that practiced at night, they always had a large squadron audience. Their leader was Lieutenant Colonel Humberto Mariles-Cortes, the very picture of south-of-the-border *machismo* as he sternly directed his officers in their nightly drill. The latter always appeared intimidated before their colonel, but were certainly bold and skillful enough over the high, wide and difficult jumps set up in the ring.

Over the years the colorful Mariles had become a familiar figure around the armory at horse show time in November and was always generous with his time and knowledge in helping the squadron horse show team in its own efforts. Alas, he came to a sorry end when his fiery temper drew him into trouble. Although eventually promoted to general, he fell from official favor when he was sentenced to ten years in prison for fatally shooting another motorist in a road rage dispute in Mexico City. He was last heard of many years later when a nightly news broadcast announced that General Mariles, the famous Mexican rider, had been arrested in France on a drug smuggling charge. A later broadcast reported his death of a heart attack in his Paris cell. *Sic transit gloria!*

Toward the end of 1949 the squadron went through another major change. The 101st Cavalry Reconnaissance Squadron (Mecz.) became the 1st Battalion of the 101st Armored Cavalry (the 2nd Battalion was formed in the Brooklyn armory) and the eventual regimental commander was Colonel William C. Roberson. An icon in Squadron A, Bill Roberson had enlisted in the squadron in 1923 and had risen to the rank of colonel as a staff officer in Europe in World War II. His return to the active squadron was warmly welcomed.

An armored cavalry regiment was something new in the army's scheme of things. Although its mission was still that of traditional cavalry–reconnaissance and security–its means were greatly expanded. The experiences of World War II had proven the need for more fire power and, as we have seen, the squadron had been enlarged to a group and had artillery and other arms and services attached to it at various times in Europe. This new concept provided for more power right within the regiment, with heavier armor and a "cannon company" as an organic part of each battalion. And there was a regimental air section as well.

While later versions of the armored cavalry regiment called for clouds of helicopters, the new Squadron A "air force" consisted of two little Piper Cub type single engine observation planes, piloted by Captains William Ennis and Charles Putnam, both men with old Squadron A family connections and World War II flying experience. Bill had been a B-24 bomber pilot in Italy, and Charlie was a former fighter pilot and aerial gunnery instructor. They brought with them a unique sense of humor and a typical Air Force nonchalance that was sometimes considered by the higher brass to be a lack of discipline. Although they had taken the grommets out of their garrison caps in traditional World War II Air Force manner, they were considered by their peers to be excellent officers, and not the least out of control. With a tip of the hat to those famous aviation pioneers, their squadron buddies had nicknamed them "Orville" and "Wilbur."

Like the planes, the armor of the new regiment was not exactly "state of the art," but that was not the point. While the tanks and half-tracks were still of World War II vintage, it was the concept of combined arms in one regimental package that was at the heart of the matter, and the squadron trained hard to meet the new requirements. The armory was the scene of individual and small unit training, Camp Smith still provided the firing ranges for weekly small arms practice and now the vast acreage of Fort Drum was just about the only military reservation in New York State big enough for the summertime maneuvering of a National Guard armored cavalry regiment.

While all the difficult staff planning and all the hard physical work of the troops was going on to meet the needs of the new reorganization, the horse activities in the armory continued–but not at their usual tempo. The Horse Troop held its weekly drills, the children's afternoon riding classes were beginning to fill, the Saturday night polo games were as popular as ever and the horse show team continued to show, both in the armory and out. Yet, due to a shortage of horses and the departure of that enthusiastic horseman, Colonel Thackeray, whose official tour of duty with the National Guard was over, there was a certain lack of organization among the squadron's horsemen. That all changed with the arrival on the scene of Lieutenant Colonel Frederick L. Devereux, Jr.

Fred Devereux had joined Squadron A in 1936, served as a lieutenant at Fort Devens and then transferred out of the 101st Cavalry to end the war as lieutenant colonel in Europe. Now, as a reserve officer, but not an active member of the regiment, he had returned to lend his time and talents to building up the riding activities and preserving the horse traditions of Squadron A. The program and rules which you will find in the appendix, drawn up by Colonel Devereux in 1949, not only demonstrate the energy he applied to the project, but give a valid picture of the last days of equestrian activity in Squadron A.

The "park card," now necessary for riding Squadron A horses in Central Park, was in itself a unique document. In addition to listing a set of strict but understandable regulations for riding in Central Park, Rule Number 5 read, "Riders will not dismount at, or frequent, the Tavern on the Green." The reason for this draconian ruling, it seems, was that sometime in the past it had become habitual for certain Squadron A troopers riding in the park to tie up their horses outside that famous New York watering hole and drop in for a little afternoon nip. Apparently, on one occasion this went a bit too far. Rumor has it that the innocent revelry turned into a donnybrook and the police were called. The final result was that Rule 5, the squadron prohibition regarding rider visits to that popular inn and New York landmark.

The squadron was having a more pleasant relationship with the police at this time, however. Now taking part in the frequent squadron schooling shows were members of the New York City Police Troop C, who patrolled Central Park and had long stabled their horses in the armory. They had organized an excellent horse show team under a Lieutenant Burke, whose Irish brogue seemed to complement his equestrian know-how. Their top horse was an athletic little jumper of indeterminate breeding named "Planter," ridden by Patrolman Joe Hill

Over the years a friendly, but continuing, rivalry had grown between the police riders and the Squadron horse show team, and although the squadron people sometimes came out ahead in the ribbons against some of the police, they seldom could beat Planter and Joe Hill. It was an embarrassing condition that existed to the very end of the squadron's horse activities, but even after that, the friendship with the police remained. Indeed, the wife of Inspector Meehan, the officer who commanded the entire New York City mounted police, kept her horse in the armory and was accorded all the squadron's privileges.

One of the last equestrian adventures of Squadron A was the tryouts in the spring of 1950 for the first civilian United States Equestrian Team. The U.S. Army horse cavalry had been disbanded by that time and with it went the Army's last horse show team. To fill the void, a group of patriotic Americans (including the squadron's own Tubby Tuckerman) banded together to back a civilian team that would represent the United States in international competition, including the Olympic Games of 1952. Selection trials for horses and riders were held throughout the country.

With an ambition that exceeded its abilities, the Squadron A horse show team entered the east coast trials, which were held at Westchester Country Club. A huge number of hopefuls from all of the east participated, riding ever imaginable type of horse, from beautiful conformation hunters to riding school hacks–including one Tennessee Walker that obviously had never seen a horse show jump before! In those days knowledge of Olympic requirements was not widespread among American horsemen.

The squadron people performed well enough, but were disappointed when they failed to make the cut. However, they took comfort from the fact that no one else did either—not one of the dozens of riders who took part in the trials was selected for the team. In fact, the only east coast rider who ended up on that first U.S. Equestrian Team was New Jersey's Arthur McCashin—and he had not even shown up for the trials! (However, it all worked out well. McCashin did a splendid job as team captain and in a few years the American civilian team had developed into one of the best in the world.)

New York being the city it is, the horse activities in the armory continued to attract horsemen from many parts of the world. Looking back, one can remember such colorful characters as 90-year-old General Alexander Rodzianko, a Russian Czarist officer who had been a famous coach of various European international horse show teams and for a short period coached the squadron horse show team. Another rider of Russian descent was Baron Alexis Wrangel, son of a famous Russian general, a member of the Squadron A Horse Troop and the horse show team. Later, while serving with an American relief organization in the Middle East, he trained with the Egyptian cavalry team, and was rumored to be a CIA agent. There was also a third Russian horseman, a kindly gentleman, an ex-Czarist colonel who was remembered for his courtly manners and for drinking hot tea out of a glass and smoking cigarettes out of an unbelievably long holder.

Another exotic rider was Prince Paul Sapieha, who held his listeners spellbound with tales of his adventures in the Polish lancers in World War I. But for exciting tales of World War II, no one could beat the ex-Canadian Sergeant Armstrong in the active National Guard. A veteran of the ill-starred Dieppe raid, he drilled his Squadron A troop as though they were British guardsmen, with bellowed commands that almost brought the armory down. There were many other picturesque types, and old-timers remembered them all.

In June of 1950, history intruded once again on the squadron's fun and games. A strong force of North Koreans crossed the 38th parallel borderline into South Korea, and the Korean War was on. This happened just as the 101st Armored Cavalry was preparing for its annual two weeks field training at Fort Drum. As might be expect, that summer encampment was quite different from the previous ones.

In Korea, the Americans rushed troops to the front to assist the Republic of Korea (ROK) Army in resisting the invasion. But the U.S. Army was as unprepared for war as their ROK allies, and they were pushed back to a tenuous perimeter at the southern end of the peninsula. Back in the States the troopers at Drum were in a high state of optimistic excitement and thought they were ready to be called up and shipped out to Korea almost as soon as summer camp was over.

It was not to be. As the war dragged on it became evident that very few elements of the National Guard would be called into federal service and the 101st Cavalry would not be one of them—at least not until its ranks were filled to war strength. So the company commanders put extra effort into recruiting, helped by a new draft law that exempted individual National Guardsmen from Selective Service in return for a longer stint in the Guard. With orders to fill the ranks, the recruiters scurried around to find prospects up to Squadron A standards. Eventually the requirements were met, and with accelerated training the regiment felt it was ready to go, the men actually believing that they would soon be on the way. This feeling was reinforced by an item in Walter Winchell's popular gossip column in the tabloid New York Daily Mirror reporting that Squadron A was about to be federalized!

Although it eventually became obvious that the 101st wasn't going anywhere, plans were nevertheless drawn up for a state guard unit to be organized in the armory should they unlikely happen. Once again the Ex-members Association would supply the cadre for the unit, to be called the 20th Internal Security Battalion, New York State Guard. Potentially, it looked like this:

>Lieutenant Colonel Edgar A. Kniffen, Battalion C.O.
>Major Charles K. Bullard, Executive Officer
>Captain Frank L. Froment, Headquarters Troop
>Captain Werner c. Bruchlos, A Troop
>Captain R. Bruce Estelle, B Troop
>Captain William Hanway, C Troop

Of course, since the National Guard was not called, the security battalions were never completely organized, but the squadron veterans were ready and willing to do their part had the occasion arisen.

The war settled into a stalemate and then came to an end in 1953. Sometime after it was over, a trooper ran into the squadron's old regular army instructor, Colonel Thackeray (at a horse show, of course), who had been wounded in Korea. When asked about the war he gave his considered verdict: "You didn't miss much. It wasn't a very good war."

But the conflict, nevertheless, had a considerable effect on Squadron A. Because the riding, and the social life that went with it, seemed trivial and was also too much added responsibility in such serious times, there was a movement by the regimental brass to get rid of the horses. And in spite of many hasty meetings, heated arguments and impassioned protests, the deed was done. The riding activities were unceremoniously cancelled and the squadron horses disappeared from the armory although the police horses stayed on and the polo continued.

The Korean War had shaken up the American military establishment, and throughout the 1950s the quickened pace of military training continued in the Squadron. That mood of military alertness was reflected in many ways, not the least of which was a surprise state callup in April 1955, called "Operation Minuteman." At that time the neighborhood around 94th Street was alarmed (and perhaps entertained) when the practice emergency alert summoned the entire 1st Battalion of the 101st Armored Cavalry to the armory, sentries were mounted around the outside of the building and tanks posted on Madison and Park Avenues. It was quite a demonstration, and the troopers took it seriously, ninety-six percent of the squadron answering the call. Even those who were out of town got the word and responded—Major John H. Neitman, executive officer of the battalion answered the call from Florida and Sergeant First Class Natt Steen reported in from Texas.

That was one of the last extensive military demonstrations involving the armory on 94th Street, for now the pot was boiling in Albany in a movement to remove most of the National Guard units from crowded Manhattan and into more modern quarters in the outlying boroughs of the big city.

CHAPTER 5. THE BIG MOVE

BY the end of the 1950's the huge, castle-like structure on Madison Avenue that stretched the entire block between 94th and 95th Streets and all the way up to Park Avenue was beginning to show its age. Known affectionately in the neighborhood as "the old Squadron A Armory," it had first been constructed as a separate building on Madison Avenue, built to house a single troop of cavalry. Then, as the troop grew into a squadron, the building was enlarged to incorporate the adjacent Eighth Regiment Armory on Park Avenue. Now, as the decade of the 1960s dawned, it was supposed to house the entire 1st Battalion of the 101st Armored Cavalry with its collection of tanks, half-tracks, self-propelled howitzers, trucks and jeeps.

To the military minds in Albany, the building was not quite up to the job. It was a magnificent structure designed and built in a great sweeping manner variously described as either "Scottish baronial" or "styled after the Chateau Gaillard in Normandy, built by Richard the Lion-Hearted." But, according to the brass, it was just no longer suited to modern military use. The grand old building was doomed.

There were several competing interests at work here. The state military authorities were interested in modernization and wanted to move several of its National Guard units to areas less constricting than the sidewalks of Manhattan. (At this time there was one other armory in Manhattan and two in Brooklyn targeted for sale or destruction.) There were also the powerful real estate interests salivating to get their hands on these rare and valuable New York City properties, particularly the prize of Squadron A's full city block on Manhattan's "Gold Coast."

But most anxious of all was the City of New York in the person of the Manhattan Borough President, Edward R. Dudley, who had visions of much-needed middle income housing in this highly desirable neighborhood. The relationship between the city and the state in this matter was a strange one. The city had originally owned both the land and the building, but under an agreement entered into at the beginning of World War II, had turned over the property to the state "for military purposes." Now they were negotiating with the state, not to buy the property back, it was explained, but simply to pay for the replacement of facilities–along with the other New York City properties, this was to the tune of some $6 million. The city would pay $2 million and it is assumed that the federal government would pick up the tab for the rest. The city would then be able to use the property for whatever purpose it wished.

This suited Borough President Dudley, but raised a howl of protest from other quarters, particularly from the residents of the neighborhood, who had grown fond of the old building and liked having the polo ponies and police horses around. Letters were written to the newspapers complaining of the potential loss of police protection in the neighborhood, and there was one letter from a six-year-old girl to Dudley himself, begging the city not to take the horses away, and explaining how much "the castle" mean to the local children.

In 1960 Squadron A, whose official designation had in 1959 become 1st Squadron, 101st NYARNG, was advised that it would have to vacate the armory before its return from the summer camp of that year. Its temporary new home would be the 69th Regiment Armory on 23rd Street and Lexington Avenue–but only while the armory on Staten Island was being prepared as its permanent residence. The spacious Staten Island property was a much more suitable training site for armor than the crowded Manhattan building, but after nearly a century in Manhattan, it was a sad move for Squadron A.

In that same year there also appeared another contender for the great prize of the Manhattan armory property. It was New York City's Board of Education, who wanted it for a new junior high school. For the next few years there were bitter battles among the city departments for rights to the building. The matter was finally settled in favor of a school and plans were drawn up for demolition of the armory to make room for construction of the new Junior High School 29. Apparently Borough President Dudley lost his bid for middle-income housing.

While all this controversy was going on, the polo and police horses had continued living and working in the armory, and another National Guard unit, the 1st Battle Group, 251st Infantry, replaced the 101st Cavalry. When it came time to vacate, it was comparatively easy to find new space for the Guard and the police, but the polo club was another matter. It was called upon to leave the property very suddenly indeed. According to the *New York Herald Tribune* of January 11, 1966, Herb Pennell, then the manager of Squadron A polo, had been told he could continue the winter season until March. Instead, he got his marching orders on January 10. As the *Tribune* put it, "The shortest season in the history of indoor polo ended yesterday."

Pennell, not without difficulty, found places for his ponies in Westchester and Long Island and the police horses were transferred to a hastily converted garage on West 55th Street near 10th Avenue. There were 57 police mounts in the armory, many of them green and in training, and they made quite a parade as they clattered across town through Central Park to their new home. After the polo ponies and police horses had departed, someone had written in chalk on the stable door of the empty armory, "And then there were none."

Three weeks later Patrolman Frank Orapello, on duty in Central Park, tied his horse, Joseph, outside the Arsenal Police Station in the park at 60th Street and entered the building. When he came out again shortly after, the horse was gone—he had slipped his tether and wandered off.

Aided by a few fellow patrolmen on horseback, Orapello searched frantically for his mount, but without success. Then he had a brainstorm. "Check the old armory," he called to his mounted friends.

Sure enough, there at the armory's stable door, waiting patiently for someone to open it, stood Joseph. Apparently the troopers of Squadron A were not the only ones who missed their old home.

By the late winder of 1966 the demolition of the great building was in full swing. The *New Yorker* magazine of March 14 of that year told the story in its "Talk of the Town" section. It had arranged for Warrant Officer Frank Mugavin, who as former assistant superintendent of the building, knew it inside and out, to meet with William Perrin, foreman of the demolition crew. Even as Mugavin was describing the stables, the ring, the Ex-members Room, the restaurant and all the other parts of the armory the troopers knew so well, the Kaiser-Nelson Steel and Salvage Company wrecking crew was taking it down.

"What will you do with all that stuff?" Mr Mugavin asked.
"Sell it," Mr. Perrin replied. "Trusses, beams, girders, pipe, roofing, copper drains—you name it and we'll dig up a customer.

Later this month, when we begin battering in the walls, we'll sell the undamaged bricks."

At this point, there was a warning shout from below, and a few seconds later the center section of a bow truss dropped to the floor of the polo field with a tremendous crash, which shook the building and sent up a cloud of dust.

"Well, I bet you never thought you'd see anything like that," Mr. Perrin said with a grin. "No, I sure didn't," Mr. Mugavin replied. "I knew the armory had become an impractical old barn, but I never thought they'd tear it down. Not in my lifetime, anyway."

That's how the *New Yorker* descried the end of the Squadron A Armory. But it was not the end of Squadron A – the Ex-members Association saw to that. Well before the demolition of the armory was begun, it was decided to maintain the club and continue the historic traditions of the squadron. A committee was formed to find a place to exhibit the memorabilia that had been collected over the years, the flags and guidons, the ribbons and trophies, the medals and decorations, the memories of more than 75 years of service to the city, state and nation.

After an exhaustive search in midtown Manhattan, the Association was fortunate in securing space in the famous Biltmore Hotel on East 43rd Street. Exclusive quarters were established in the luxurious old library, a spacious room paneled in dark English oak under a beautifully decorated tray ceiling with hand-made chandeliers of German silver. It was to be the headquarters of Squadron A for some 15 years, until the Biltmore was converted to an office building.

There was a great party to celebrate the opening of the new clubroom. The following is the report, in part of that celebration from the next day's *New York Herald Tribune*:

THE HORSELESS SQUADRON A
by Ralph Chapman

"It's a lovely place," said one of the older members, "but it doesn't smell the same."

He was stating a fact.

The first Squadron A Horse Show Team to be organized after World War II. (L to R) Dave Munroe on Stormy Weather, a Squadron horse; Ed Bimberg on Hussar, another Squadron horse; Alex Wrangel on a horse loaned by Colonel Thackeray; George Hoblin on his own mount; and Bill Sherman on a Squadron horse.

Practice makes perfect. Even after a hard day's work at the office, the various members of the horse show team would often gather in the Armory for a short period of practice. The regular sessions were on Wednesdays, but the jumpers would fit their workouts wherever they could—weekends, too.

Ed Bimberg on Zip, riding for the Squadron A Horse Show Team in the early 1950s. This was in one of the local shows in the Armory leading up to the big Squadron A Spring Horse Show that attracted competitors from all over the East.

Reward enough for the hard work of training jumping horses were the ribbons won at the frequent local schooling shows held in the Armory. Here, in an evening show, Ed Bimberg takes Hopeful over the course.

WILLIAM SHATNER RECEIVING SQUADRON A AWARD FROM LINDA AND BOB MCLEAN AND BOBBY DURYEA AT THE NATIONAL HORSE SHOW.

Squadron A Club at the Biltmore Hotel

SQUADRON A

The Biltmore does not smell like the Squadron A Armory on upper Park Avenue. The reason is that its guests do not include horses.

But the old armory is being torn down to make way for a school and the 62-year-old Association of Ex-members of Squadron A, now 2,000 strong, had to find new quarters. They are now in residence at the Biltmore, in the paneled room known as "the library."

When the new clubroom was opened officially last week, some 400 members and their guests from all over the country assembled for a party. Nostalgia was the order of the night. Memories ran from the "horse cavalry" of Mexican border days to indoor polo with the country's greatest players competing on the immense expanse between Park and Madison Avenues and 94th and 95th Streets.

There was some grumbling that Squadron A had seemed in recent years to be known more as a polo club than as a National Guard unit whose members fought from San Juan Hill through both World Wars. Actually the squadron was disbanded as a horse troop in 1951 and has not mounted a polo team of its own since then, except in the 1980s; Peter Tcherpinene started a Squadron A polo team which competed at Mashomach Club at Milbrook New York for several years.

Allen Evarts Foster, now 80 but still long and lean as any trooper in the movies or on TV and still practicing law in New York, turned up for the party and talked of other days.

"I joined the squadron on February 18, 1910, my 25th birthday," he recalled, and I still remember the officer who swore me in.

"You're a free man now," but when you take this oath you serve your country for five years.

"I'd never been on a horse in my life and, believe me, the first time I had to go near one I was more scared than I ever was later in combat in World War I."

"Now," he said, unfolding himself from an armchair and grasping his cane, "where's the bar?"

While the furnishings and memorabilia of the Ex-members Room could easily be moved to the new quarters, the great bronze World War I Memorial Gate, which had been erected in the squad room in the armory, could not. Once again the Ex-members Association, in the persons of Bill Roberson, Tubby Tuckerman and Clarence Michalis, went to work. They got the state's permission to remove the gates from the armory and, after prolonged negotiation, found an appropriate place to erect them.

The new location was in the Church of the Heavenly Rest on Fifth Avenue and 91st Street. It was altogether fitting that this beautiful place of worship be the background for the impressive memorial to the squadron dead of the first World War, for the annual Squadron A church parade had been held at Heavenly Rest for the previous 76 years, and a yearly memorial service continues to this day.

In the meanwhile, the battle of the armory between the city and the public went on. Even while the walls were coming down protests against the demolition filled the newspapers. Finally someone suggested that the Madison Avenue wall and the two massive towers on either end be left standing as an historical gateway to the proposed school's playground. The city Landmarks Preservation Commission was brought into the act.

It was all in the newspapers. The *New York Times* of August 9, 1966 put it this way:

CITY MAY SAVE PIECE OF "CASTLE"; LAST WALL OF 94TH STREET ARMORY

by Bernadette Carey

Children who live in the east 90's near Madison and Park Avenues may not completely lose their "castle," the old Squadron A Armory at 94th Street and Park. The armory is being torn down to make room for a junior high school, but the city agencies, responding to pleas of the area residents, may leave standing the last remaining wall with its turrets and battlements.

The neighborhood's residents waged a losing battle last year to save all the old building, where the National Guard drilled, the mounted police once housed their horses and where polo was played.

But the preservation of one wall has interested the Landmarks Preservation Committee, the Board of Education and the Mayor's Office.

Eugene E. Hult, Executive Director of the Office of School Buildings for the Board of Education, said last week that his office was looking at the possibility of incorporating the wall into the design of the new school's playground.

"So far we see no real problem in trying to save it for our children," he said.

Also under consideration, he added, are plans for developing classrooms or play areas in the towers and perhaps adding some sort of museum.

Alan Burnham, executive director of the Landmarks preservation Commission, said, "We think it's a fine building, so we are working with other agencies involved in its disposal."

Michael Dontzin, special counsel to the Mayor, said, "There have been innumerable suggestions from people in the neighborhood to save the armory."

"The Landmarks Preservation Commission asked the Mayor's office to help save the wall, which is part of the building's original structure," he report. "What we've done is to temporarily stop its demolition while we try to find out if it's practical to save it."

On October 11, 1966 the Landmarks Preservation Commission held a public hearing on the matter. As a result, twelve witnesses spoke in favor the designation of the armory wall as a landmark, while four spoke against it, reasoning that it might delay the construction of the school. Some comments in favor of maintaining the wall were strong indeed.

A representative of the Historic Buildings Committee of the American Institute of Architects, New York chapter, testified, saying that he "urges this commission to do all it can to preserve these remains," and that "what remains today is dear to us in its own right. Of that, especially the towers with the machicolated parapets, their rounded turrets and corbeled galleries, we who have studied and practiced architecture find of particular aesthetic merit, their color, their massing, their interesting silhouettes, their detail and their beautifully executed brickwork. We are of the opinion these towers and connecting wall provide an effective background for the school to be, and a romantic background for those using the playground.

The representative of the City Park Department testified that, "the facade is an example of a type of Military Gothic architecture and workmanship, which is no longer being built in New York City and which will probably disappear entirely from the urban scene. The design is of a type which will without doubt provide a tremendous amount of delight to the small children who will play in the playground of the newly proposed school. The castle effect which the wall creates certainly provides an enormously varied setting for all forms of play. We are in favor of preserving the facade."

A decision was not long in coming. It read:

FINDINGS AND DESIGNATIONS

On the basis of careful consideration of the history, the architecture and other features of this building, the Landmarks Preservation Commission finds that the Madison Avenue front (including corner towers) of the Squadron A Armory has a special character, special historical and aesthetic interest and value as part of the development, heritage and cultural characteristics of New York City.

The Commission further finds that, among its important qualities, the Madison Avenue front (including corner towers) of the Squadron A Armory is an outstanding example of military architecture, that is notable for its massive size and bold detail, that it is a fine example of masonry construction, and that of its type it is one of the few remaining examples of regimental armories in New York City.

Accordingly, pursuant to the provisions of Chapter 8-A of the Charter of the City of New York and Chapter 8-A of the Administrative Code of the City of New York, the Landmark Preservation Commission designates as a Landmark the Madison Avenue front (including corner towers) of the Squadron A Armory, Madison Avenue between 94th and 95th Streets, Borough of Manhattan, and designates as a Landmark the Madison Avenue front (including corner towers) of the Squadron A Armory, Madison Avenue between 94th and 95th Streets, Borough of Manhattan, and designates as its related Landmark Site that part of Borough of Manhattan Tax Block Map, Block

1506, Lot 21 which contains the land on which the described improvement is situated.

So, in that important respect, Squadron A lives on in perpetuity, as a monumental Madison Avenue gateway to whatever will lie behind it.

That's the good news.

The bad news is that although the proposed high school was eventually erected at the Park Avenue end of the property, in spite of all the ballyhoo no playground has ever been constructed. The old Squadron A Armory wall has been standing guard for at least 35 years (at the present writing) over a huge, rubble-filled hole in the ground. We can only hope that some use can eventually be made of that valuable property, some function appropriate to its splendid history.

If the site of the old armory was shamefully neglected, the history and traditions of Squadron A were not. From the opening of the clubrooms in the Biltmore in 1965 through the next four decades, great care was taken to ensure that the memories and memorabilia of the squadron were preserved in a suitably respectful venue. The changeover from armory to clubroom was not easy. It was a job taken up by the E-members Association with enthusiasm, but there came a point after the move of the active National Guard regiment to Staten Island when it became obvious that there would be fewer and fewer old Squadron A men left to carry on.

Eventually, after much discussion, it was decided to change the charter of the association and open the membership to other than former Squadron A troopers. The name of the organization was changed from "Ex-members" to simply "Squadron A Association, Incorporated," and certain new categories of membership were added. These included a Family Membership for relatives of those already members, and an Associate Membership for those non-members sponsored by a member.

How successful this new concept became can be judged by the activities of the Squadron A Association in the years following the demolition of the armory. In the late 1960s and throughout the 1970s the Association sponsored a series of what might be called "entertainments" for members and their guests. These featured as speakers a list of prominent figures in the military, political and sporting worlds. Among these were such diverse personalities as

Allen Dulles, World War II spy master and later director of the CIA, and Thomas W. "Tim" Durant, the "galloping grandfather," who rode in two of the famous (and very dangerous) Grand National steeplechase races at Aintree, England, when he was almost 70 years of age.

Another well-received speaker was ex-member Whitman Knapp, whose name was at that time frequently in the newspapers. A prominent Manhattan attorney, he was chairman of the group of distinguished citizens known as the Knapp Commission that was investigating the then widespread corruption in the New York City Police Department. The results of that inquiry were so sensational that they became a book and then a popular motion picture called "Serpico," the name of the principal witness and hero of the case, and the Knapp Commission became famous countrywide. White was later appointed a federal judge and continued the important work of helping to root out corruption in government.

Within that same time frame the squadron also sponsored three European summer tours, each with the Dublin Horse Show as its centerpiece, and each led by former K Troop member Lieutenant Colonel Ed Maher. One highlight of the 1969 trip was a delightful cocktail party given for the Squadron A group at the American Embassy in Dublin's Phoenix Park by Ambassador John D.J. Moore— who happened to be a former Squadron A trooper himself!

Later squadron tours included side trips to London, Copenhagen, the Norwegian fjords and Paris, but all were centered around the fabulous Dublin show. In Dublin the squadron visitors were treated royally by the Irish cavalry at their headquarters in McKee Barracks in Phoenix Park. There they were entertained at the Irish Cavalry Club and had the honor of being inducted as honorary members. They were also conducted around the stables and shown the famous Irish team jumpers, a particular treat for the horse-loving old troopers of the squadron.

Back in New York, the Squadron continued sponsoring social activities right through the 1970s, beginning with trips to the Fairfield Hunt club in Connecticut for the annual Squadron A Polo Day series of polo games arranged by ex-member George Haas who had been on the Squadron A polo team until the very end of armory polo. Other Squadron A excursions of that era featured visits to Warrenton, Virginia to enjoy a weekend at the Virginia Gold Cup steeplechase races, and to Glyndon, Maryland for that most prestigious of all amateur races over fences, the Maryland Hunt Cup. All the while the social life at the Biltmore clubrooms carried on unabated, and the squadron veterans of the Mexican Border and World War I 105th Machine Gun Battalion maintained their cherished reunions.

But events weren't all wine and roses for Squadron A. In 1981 it lost its beloved home. The historic Biltmore Hotel was converted to an office building and the squadron found itself out in the cold. But not for long – the hard-working officers and committee members got busy and, after much searching, new clubrooms were found in the Chemists' Club on east 41st Street. The new quarters provided a congenial atmosphere in a convenient neighborhood and the troopers were right at home in short order. Of course, the move required a great deal of work, both physical and administrative, much of the credit for which should go to Harriet Heubsch, the club's longtime Executive Director, as well as to the various committees involved.

But there was one more move in store for the Association. In 1988 the Chemists Club closed down and Squadron A was once again out in the cold. The situation was desperate. After losing its beautiful home in the Biltmore, this further loss was a fearful blow. The club's membership had slipped from 1400 to less than 700, and there was some doubt as to its survival.

The members of the Executive Committee once again rolled up their sleeves and started a search for new quarters throughout the desirable section of midtown Manhattan from 34th Street to 50th Street, the Gold Coast, for clubhouse convenience. But despite a painstaking investigation of some 27 possible sites, nothing suitable could be found.

A crisis was averted, however, when the most recent president of the Association, Colonel Robert L. McLean, suggested looking into the Women's National Republican Club at 3 West 51st Street. The WNRC had everything the squadron was looking for–a convenient midtown location off Fifth Avenue, unbeatable facilities and just the right atmosphere. Alas, however, there was no room! But the fact that Mildred McLean, Bob's mother, had at one time been Executive Director of the WNRC, must have had some influence, because the club's president (whose husband, incidentally, was a West Pointer) ordered her manager to *make* room. The deed was done and the move was made. Both clubs benefited and it proved a successful arrangement. Squadron A had the use of a beautiful clubhouse which now included, as part of the restaurant, a bard decorated in squadron style with cavalry mementos and even an oil painting of General Roe that had once hung on the wall of the Ex-Members' Room in the old armory on Madison Avenue.

Of course, there were many more changes after the move to the WNRC. The sale of a valuable Remington bronze owned by the squadron provided the seed money for a "Squadron A Fund" that was created to support horse-related activities. Among the organizations that subsequently received financial assistance from the fund were the United States Cavalry Association, the 101st Cavalry Museum, the United States Equestrian Team, the United States Military Equestrian Team, the National Horse Sports Foundation, the ASPCA, the American Horse Protection Association and several organizations that support therapeutic riding for handicapped children. The New York Community Trust was selected to manage this fund.

Another charitable fund called the "Squadron A Foundation" was created to support a wider range of causes, emphasizing the military and, particularly, the cavalry. Using money from this source, the squadron provided five $500 college scholarships to soldiers of the 101st Cavalry. Their commanding officer reported that not only was the gift greatly appreciated by the recipients, but the Squadron A veterans' recognition of the active organization raised the morale of the entire unit.

During this period there were many new events added to the list of squadron entertainments, everything from a yearly anniversary party on the aircraft carrier *U.S.S. Intrepid,* now a museum tied up alongside a Hudson River pier, to a "Sports Art Cocktail Party" at the famous Sotheby's auction house in mid-Manhattan. While these reflected the "polo and party" days of the old squadron, there was a more military aura about such other outings as the visit to the Aberdeen Proving Ground in Maryland to shoot the M1 Abrams tank and the M2 Bradley fighting vehicle and firing the pistol on the range at the armory on Staten Island–all fun and games for Squadron A members.

And thanks to the close relationship between the Squadron and the WNRC, reciprocal arrangements were made with other select clubs throughout the country and, indeed, throughout the world. Now squadron members could find comfortable, even luxurious, accommodations in many outstanding venues all over.

SQUADRON A CLUB QUARTERS
IN THE WOMEN'S NATIONAL REPUBLICAN CLUB BUILDING
3 WEST 51ST STREET, NEW YORK, NY 10019

Much of the success in managing the Squadron A Association's business is due to the untiring efforts of Executive Director Harriet Huebsch. Here she is shown with Bob McLean, behind the scenes during Belmont Park Racetrack's Squadron A Day, 1998.

101st Cavalry Armory, Staten Island

Colonel Bob McLean with M-1 Tank, today's 101st Cavalry equipment

CHAPTER 6. ACROSS THE BAY

THE charter of the Squadron A Association states that among the particular objects for which it is formed is to "encourage the active organization in every way in its power." Many thought that this relationship would be lost when the armory was torn down and the active National Guard unit moved across the bay to Staten Island.

But these naysayers were wrong. The ties between Squadron A and the National Guard on Staten Island are now as strong as ever—and, in fact, this relationship has had a long history. Before World War II the 101st Cavalry and the 121st Cavalry of upstate New York formed the 51st Cavalry Brigade—and brigade headquarters was in that same Staten Island armory. Moreover, the brigade commander was Brigadier General N. Hiller Egleston, who had commanded Squadron A from 1919 through 1932, and was president of the Ex-Members Association in 1946. So it seems that the connection between the club in Manhattan and the tank battalion on Staten Island is older than some may have realized.

It took a little time for the 1st Squadron, 101st Cavalry to settle down in its new home and, as the reconnaissance Squadron of the 42nd (Rainbow) Division, it shared all the changes in military thinking of the next few decades. Over the years its light tanks and scout cars were superceded by the might M1 "Abrams" 60-ton main battle tanks and its World War II jeeps became the versatile HMMWV, the "Humvees" used as everything from heavily armed patrol and reconnaissance vehicles to ambulances. And in the air the original two Piper Cub type two-seater monoplanes developed into two troops of helicopters, stationed upstate.

While this transformation was going on, the training became more intense and varied. As the army developed the principle of air-land warfare to meet the increasing challenge of the Soviets in the cold war the National Guard became important in the concept of the "total army." The 101st Cavalry led the way, taking part in combined-arms live fire exercises at Fort Drum, practicing advanced tank gunnery over newly constructed ranges and conducting large scale river crossing maneuvers, no mean feat considering the size and complexity of the squadron's equipment.

In the summer maneuvers of 1989 the 101st actually held joint exercises at the Canadian Army Forces Base at Gagetown, New Brunswick. The tanks were shipped there on navy landing craft, loading at Staten Island and the Port of Albany. As a demonstration of inter-service and international cooperation the exercises were a tremendous success and once more proved the military efficiency of the 101st Cavalry.

Less than half of the National Guard was mobilized for the Gulf War, but the squadron did its part. It was called up early for its usual field training and, instead of Fort Drum, it was sent to the National Training Center at Fort Irwin, California. There it did yeoman duty in acting as the "enemy" in desert maneuvers that prepared Regular Army troops for war.

The gulf War proved the efficacy of the Army's theories of armored warfare in the desert, but it hardly prepared the 101st Cavalry for the role it was to play in its quite unscheduled call-up a decade later. In between those years the usual summer field training at Drum and the weekend drills at the armory kept the Squadron on its toes.

While all this unusually intense training was going on, the squadron managed to maintain its role in local civic activities and regimental duties. The active unit is always a participant in the annual Memorial Day parade on Staten Island, and has taken part in the Armed Forces Week Parade up Fifth Avenue in Manhattan, where the tanks and armored personnel carriers made a big hit with the crowd.

Each year the unit holds Memorial Day services on the grounds of the armory and the troops turn out before a large audience. There are tributes paid to the honored dead of the 101st Cavalry in addresses by the commanding officer and a number of distinguished guests, including state legislators and civic leaders. A firing squad fires the traditional three volleys and a wreath is laid. It is a moving ceremony, followed by a march past of the troops and a reception in the armory. Each year a delegation from the Squadron A Association attends and is warmly welcomed.

Another memorial to the 101st Cavalry is permanently installed at the U.S. Army's Armor School at Fort Knox, Kentucky. It is in the form of an obelisk, with inscriptions on three of its four sides—a dedication to the machine-gun battalions of World War I; a listing of the various official designations by which the 101st Cavalry has been known down through the years, an honor role of its eight campaigns, from Puerto Rico in 1898 to Central Europe in 1945, plus its Mexican Border service in 1916. It is a fitting tribute and an everlasting one.

Another landmark in the history of the 101st Cavalry was the dedication of the "Cavalry Room" in the Staten Island Armory in 1981. It is a regimental museum that includes paintings of former commanders, cups and ribbons won for riflery and horsemanship down through the years, uniforms, medals, weapons and a host of other militaria.

According to Lieutenant Colonel Robert Wedinger, who was commanding officer of the Squadron during the museum's construction, plans were originally made "directed specifically to the preservation of the lineage of the 101st Cavalry and to unit veterans. Artifacts were at a premium, funds non-existent and trophies in disrepair. Once again we sounded the bugle, a call to all present and past members and friends, to respond to the assistance of our unit. The response was outstanding. It solidified once again; cavalrymen can never forget their heritage. The museum was completed at a cost of $18,000 plus. Not a penny was spent on labor and materials were purchased at cost."

Needless to say, Squadron A cooperated to the fullest, contributing many military artifacts that had long decorated the Manhattan armory and subsequent clubrooms. These included everything from a beautiful painting of General Roe, the first commander of what was to become the 101st Cavalry, to cups won by the squadron in horse shows and shooting matches, as well as polo mallets and jerseys worn by the polo teams. A particularly touching exhibit to those who knew him was a photograph of Werner "Boots" Bossong in the traditional Squadron A hussar uniform, just as he looked when he led the Horse Troop down Fifth Avenue in New York City's 300th year Centennial Parade in 1950. Tragically, "Boots" was killed in a riding accident in the armory not long after the photo was taken.

The 101st Cavalry wound up the decade of the 1980's with a celebration of the 100th Anniversary (1889-1989) of the parent organization, Squadron A, at the armory on Staten Island. It was a huge success, with veterans of Squadron A and Squadron C attending, some of them traveling long distances from many parts of the country to join in the celebration.

Squadron A gave a large party on the U.S. Intrepid aircraft carrier with a U.S. Army band and the fifes and drums of the Veteran Corps of Artillery along with their 75-millimeter gun salutes. Also, there were fly-bys by biplanes.

The decade of the 1990's came with another reunion, this time of veterans of the regiment's call to federal service a half century before on January 27, 1941. The venue was the Seventh Regiment Armory, and to many the intervening years seemed not to have occurred at all. The celebrants were imbued with the spirit of the cavalry as the old times at Fort Devens were recalled, memories no doubt helped along by the free flowing social lubricants at hand. Again, it was a great success.

As we have seen, in the 1980's and early 1990's the Staten Island troops carried on the reputation of the 101st Cavalry as a crack military unit, recognized as such by the powers that be. Then, in the middle of the 1990's, it was shaken by a crisis–because of the "reduction in forces" policies in Washington at that time, it suddenly faced annihilation!

It seems that the state had to make a decision between the elimination of the 101st Cavalry in New York City or the 210th Armor, the "Palace Guard," in Albany. For months the result was uncertain and every effort was made locally to swing the balance in favor of the Staten Island unit–there were even bumper stickers that read, "Save the 101st!"

Then, as had so often happened in the past, the Squadron A Association came to the rescue of the active unit. A few wires were pulled in Washington and, after a long campaign, Bill Dunham, chairman of the Association's Executive Committee, convinced Senator Strom Thurmond, chairman of the Senate Armed Services Committee, himself a World War II Major General, to go to bat for the squadron. He reminded the Senator of the long history of the 101st and its excellent record as a military unit. He emphasized its continuous service to the nation from 1889 through the Spanish-American War, the Mexican border service and World Wars I and II.

The Senator responded. He used his immense influence with the Army to retain the squadron as a tank battalion in the 42nd Division. Also playing a prominent role was Lieutenant Colonel Leonid Kondratiuk of the National Guard Bureau, a longtime friend of Squadron A. The deed was done, the name history and battle honors were saved and the unit continues to serve as the 1st Battalion, 101st Cavalry (Tank), New York Army National Guard.

It was a close call but a fortunate one, for not many years later the unbelievable happened and the hijacked airliners of the Al Qaeda terrorists crashed into the twin towers of the World Trade Center in Manhattan. The 101st Cavalry was needed—and it was ready.

"Ready" is only a comparative term, however, for the blow was totally unexpected. No one in the city, state or federal government had the slightest idea that a gang of suicidal assassins had plans against the United States. Perhaps the American authorities should have known, in view of the bombing attempt against the building a few years before, and the more recent bombings of the U.S. embassies in Africa. But if anyone was asleep at the switch, it was not the 101st Cavalry.

As soon as the news of what had happened was broadcast, Lieutenant Colonel Mario Costagliola, commanding officer of the 101st on Staten Island, was sure his battalion would be needed, for it was one of the nearest Guard units to the scene. He tried to call Guard headquarters in Latham, N.Y., but could not get through—some New York telephone relay stations had been damaged in the attack and many of the phone lines were out. Cell phones, too, were almost useless and what was left of the system was overloaded with calls. Acting on his own, Colonel Costagliola ordered the battalion personnel officer, Captain David Willis to load a truck with medical supplies and take two ambulances and 25 troopers, including as many medics as he could gather together, and get into Manhattan as quickly as possible.

Upon arrival at the scene of what was later to be called "ground zero," Captain Willis found total confusion; at first he couldn't even find anyone in charge. Great clouds of smoke and dust were coming out of the wreckage of the buildings, irritating the lungs and stinging the eyes, and it was feared that other buildings might collapse. Soon, however, as other Guard units arrived, including three more companies of the 101st Cavalry from upstate New York, some order was brought out of the chaos. Liaison was established with the New York City Police and Fire Departments, and the Guard units were organized to provide perimeter security and traffic control. Later the 101st was given the important task of providing security for the bridges and tunnels that lead in and out of New York City and Colonel Costagliola found himself guarding the vital transportation links of one of the greatest cities in the world.

AT EASE IN THE CLUBROOMS.
STANDING (L TO R) DICK BLACK AND AN UNIDENTIFIED TROOPER.
SEATED (L TO R) GENERALS HARRY DISSTON AND BILL ROBERSON.

MG GEORGE BARKER AND VICE-PRESIDENT COL. GEORGE RENTSCHLER HEADED
FOR SQUADRON A SHOOTING EVENT AT LONG ISLAND WYANDANCH CLUB.

SQUADRON A PARTY ON THE *INTREPID*.
BOB MCLEAN AND MG JOHN KOHLER AND GUESTS.

TREASURER GEORGE RENTSCHLER AND PRESIDENT BOB MCLEAN AT THE
INTREPID AIRCRAFT CARRIER PARTY.

BILL DUNHAM AND BOB MCLEAN AT THE SQUADRON A MUSEUM.
NOTE THE DICKIE-BIRD INSIGNIAS ABOVE.

The connection between the active unit, the 101st Cavalry, and the Squadron A Association was highlighted by the appearance of men in camouflage BDU's (Battle Dress Uniform) at the Association's annual Christmas celebration in Manhattan in 2001. These were men of the 101st Cavalry who were taking a short break from the 9/11 call-up duties and enjoying the hospitality of Squadron A. They were warmly welcomed at the clubhouse party, and Colonel Costagliola addressed the celebrants, thanking the Association for its cooperation with the active unit, particularly for the college scholarship help financed by the Squadron A Foundation.

The 101st Cavalry, however, was not the only 9/11 emergency unit with a link to Squadron A. The National Guard's 53rd Troop Command was senior to all the Guard battalions on the scene; it was commanded by Brigadier General Edward G. Klein, a former C.O. of the 101st Cavalry and, of course, a member of the Squadron A Association. He was promoted to Major General and made commander of the New York Army National Guard. He points out that four former commanders of the 101st Cavalry have become general officers. That is a remarkable and unprecedented record.

The events in that dark September in the year 2001 pointed up not only the close ties between the active unit and the Association, but also the mutual determination to preserve the history and heritage of Squadron A and the 101st Cavalry. It was another step in that close relationship that has existed throughout the years.

APPENDIX I

ROSTER OF SQUADRON A OFFICERS
(as of federalization, January 27, 1941)

<u>Headquarters, Second Squadron</u>
Major William C. Roberson
Major Alfred G. Tuckerman
Captain George C. Comstock, Jr.
1st Lieutenant Wyllys Terry, Jr.

<u>Troop A</u>
Captain Edgerton Merrill
1st Lieutenant Lawrence Larkin
1st Lieutenant Frederick S. Platt
2nd Lieutenant Henry J. Brock
2nd Lieutenant Charles T. Holmes
2nd Lieutenant Frederick L. Devereux, Jr.

<u>Troop D</u>
Captain J. Noel Macy
1st Lieutenant Dexter S. French
2nd Lieutenant Theodore L. Eastmond
2nd Lieutenant Donald MacG. MacWillie
2nd Lieutenant Halsey S. Downer
2nd Lieutenant Wallace C. Reidell

<u>Troop E</u>
Captain Herbert Martin
1st Lieutenant Cornelius Perry, 2nd
1st Lieutenant Robert Ranlet, Jr.
2nd Lieutenant Milton C. Klugh
2nd Lieutenant John L. Cooper
2nd Lieutenant William W. Prout
2nd Lieutenant David C. Burton
2nd Lieutenant Theodore W. Liese

APPENDIX II

WITH THE 101ST CAVALRY IN WORLD WAR II
1940-1945

by
Colonel Charles K. Graydon

Table of Contents

Foreword
Introduction
Section
- 1 The Age of Mechanization Begins
- 2 Call to Active Duty
- 3 Fort Devens – Carolina – Pine Camp
- 4 Eastern Defense Command
- 5 Camp Campbell and Overseas Deployment
- 6 England and Movement to France
- 7 Situation on the Western Front – February 1945
  Map I – Area of Operations 7 February to 30 March
- 8 Fighting on the Line of the Saar River
- 9 Advance to the Rhine Bridgehead
  Map II – Area of Operations 31 March to 8 May
- 10 Battles along the Tauber River
- 11 Advance to the Danube
  Map III – Area of Operations 24 April to 8 May
- 12 From the Danube to the Alps
- 13 The Last Days of the War
- 14 Occupation Duty

Annex A – The Remarkable Adventures of Major French
Annex B – Officers' Roster – March 1945

DDE

GETTYSBURG
PENNSYLVANIA 17325
October 24, 1966

Dear General Tuckerman:

Thank you very much for your complimentary invitation for me to accept an Honorary Membership in Squadron A. I would be proud to accept and am happy to know that in doing so I shall be joining General Crittenberger who has been my friend since cadet days.

While I rarely get to New York and therefore will have little opportunity to visit your Club quarters, I hope you will extend to all your associates the sense of distinction I feel in your kind invitation.

With very best wishes,

Sincerely,

Dwight D. Eisenhower

Major General Alfred G. Tuckerman
U.S.A.R. Retired
Chairman Executive Committee
Association of Ex-Members of Squadron A
Biltmore Hotel
New York, New York 10017

STROM THURMOND
SOUTH CAROLINA

COMMITTEES
ARMED SERVICES, CHAIRMAN
JUDICIARY
VETERANS' AFFAIRS

United States Senate
WASHINGTON, DC 20510-4001

PRESIDENT PRO TEMPORE
UNITED STATES SENATE

September 10, 1997

Colonel Robert L. McLean
President
Squadron A Association Inc.
3 West 51st Street
New York, New York 20054

Dear Colonel McLean:

    Thank you for recent correspondence containing information regarding the Squadron A Association. I would be proud to accept your invitation to become an Honorary Member of Squadron A. It is a privilege to be able to serve the people of our great Nation. Yet, nothing is more rewarding than helping and supporting those who have chosen to wear the uniform in defense of our freedom.

    As you may be aware, I served with the Army during World War II. On D-day I was attached to the 82nd Airborne division and went on to serve with the Liberation Army in Europe. These experiences have helped me have an understanding of the sacrifices that our service people and their families have to make.

    Thank you for allowing me to be apart of your fine organization. If I can ever be of assistance, please do not hesitate to call upon me.

    With kindest regards and best wishes.

        Sincerely

        Strom Thurmond

        Strom Thurmond

INTRODUCTION

THE long line of cavalry slowly wound its way westward through softly rolling country toward the setting sun. The entire column could be seen intermittently as it crested hills and then partially disappeared at the lower elevations.

The colonel commanding and his staff rode at the head of the column closely followed by the national and regimental colors side-by-side. Behind, the red and white troop guidons flapped in the breeze at intervals down the line. The only sounds were that of cavalry in motion—creaking saddle leather, jingle of curb chains, the faint rattle of mess kits and the muffled sound of hooves as they struck the ground, accented by sharper noises as they glanced off rocks.

Each trooper wore the campaign hat with yellow hat cord, khaki shirt and breeches, boots and spurs. A Colt .45 cal. automatic hung at his belt. On each McClelland saddle hung his saddle bags, bedroll and raincoat. Each horse wore the cavalry bit and bridoon bridle and a halter with halter shank. A Springfield Model 1903 rifle hung in its scabbard on the horse's off side. The Philips pack saddles of the machine gun platoon of each rifle troop carried the Browning light machine gun while those of the machine gun troop carried the water-cooled heavy machine gun.

It was a sight to excite the mind and warm the heart of any cavalryman. This was not a scenario for a western. It was a firsthand description of the 101st Cavalry during its last field training exercise before going into federal service. The time was August 1940 and the place upper New York state near the little town of Canton. Many there had a premonition that they would never see a full regiment of horse cavalry on the march again.

It was six years and ten months later that the columns of the 101st Cavalry, thinned by casualties, presented an entirely different picture. After the surrender of the German army in May 1945 the tired, dirty units pulled out of the line in the Bavarian Alps to assembly areas in the rear. The work they had trained so long for was over.

In the following pages I have attempted to fill the gap between these two events. The period 1940 through 1944 was written from a facing memory, a few notes and records and with the help of several friends. Certain facts and dates may be in error but the story is essentially true.

Fortunately, Jack Langridge, Operations Sergeant of the 101st Cavalry brought back copies of all the operations orders and message logs of the group which he gave to me. Using them and a copy of "Wingfoot – Official History of the 101st Cavalry Group," I have been able to add an accurate narrative of the combat period to the previous four years of federal service.

My qualifications to do this are not because of a writing capability but for 12 eventful years the 101st was a second home to me, having served as an enlisted man and officer in five of the different horse and mechanized units and, finally, as group operations officer during the fighting in Europe. I was fortunate to live several summers at that veritable Bachelor's Paradise, the Squadron C Horse Farm at Huntington, L.I. and was privileged to ride on the last Squadron C polo team in 1940. After spending many years in the Army thereafter the 101st Cavalry was still "my outfit."

Charles K. Graydon
Col., Armor (Retired)

SECTION 1

THE AGE OF MECHANIZED CAVALRY BEGINS

IN 1933 General Douglas MacArthur, then Army Chief of Staff, had directed that each branch mechanize to the greatest extent needed to best execute its mission. As a result, the 1st and 13th Cavalry Regiments were dismounted and experimentally mechanized. Later, infantry tank battalions and field artillery units were merged into them to form a Provisional Armored Corps. No army had done this before.

Some of the most interested foreign military observers at the exercises and maneuvers of these units were German officers. It is not by coincidence that only a few years later the mechanized combined arms teams of the German Panzer divisions rode roughshod through the Polish cavalry and later through the entire French and British armies. The 101st Cavalry had its own sad experience with mechanized forces in the 1939 First Army maneuvers at Plattsburg, New York. Faced against the Provisional Armored Corps it was no match for such an organization. To many young cavalrymen "the handwriting was on the wall."

Beginning in 1939 most of the many National Guard cavalry regiments were transformed into horse-mechanized units (one horse squadron and one mechanized squadron). This was an apparent compromise between horse-loving senior officers and those who wished for modernization.

SECTION 2

CALL TO ACTIVE DUTY - NOVEMBER 1940

IN 1940 because of the deteriorating world situation, president Franklin Roosevelt called 100,000 National Guardsmen into federal service for a one-year period. At that time the 101st Cavalry was located in Manhattan (Squadron A), Brooklyn (Squadron C) and upstate New York (Geneseo Troop). Headquarters was in Brooklyn.

The regiment was alerted for active duty in the fall of 1940 and was reorganized from a horse regiment into a horse-mechanized regiment set up as follows:

    Regimental Headquarters
    HQ. Troop
    Service Troop
    1st Squadron (horse)
        Troops A, B, C (rifle troops)
    2nd Squadron (mechanized)
        Troops D & E (scout cars)
        Troop F (motorcycle

The service troop was equipped with enough large tractor-trailers to move the entire 1st Squadron on road marches.

As could be expected, those who were "unhorsed" and went to the mechanized units were extremely unhappy. They continued to wear boots and breeches and were authorized to wear spurs when in uniform off-duty.

During National Guard service some of the horses were supplied by the government, but most were owned by the units and rented out to Uncle Sam. When the unit went on active duty these horses, like the men, were federalized.

At any rate, the reorganization and alert orders created a frenzy of activity in the armories. In December, several lieutenants were put on active duty to attend the U.S. Cavalry School at Fort Riley to learn how to be better horse cavalry platoon leaders—horse cavalry tactics, pistol charges, horse shoeing, horsemanship, etc. With every cavalry regiment in the army soon to be or already reorganized as horse-mechanized units, we could not understand why the three-month course included only one-hour orientation in the new organization!

SECTION 3

FORT DEVENS – CAROLINAS – PINE CAMP

THE regiment was federalized on 27 January 1941 at the home armories and immediately moved to Fort Devens, Massachusetts. There it was assigned to VI Corps, U.S. First Army. At that time Colonel Gilbert Ackerman was in command with Major Alfred (Tubby) Tuckerman in command of the 1st (horse) Squadron and Major Walter Lee in command of the 2nd (mechanized Squadron.

The first weeks at Devens were spent in intensive individual training and processing of new equipment and horses. However, shortages, particularly of vehicles, horses and radios handicapped training for many months.

In the meanwhile the wives who followed their men had their first experience as camp followers, the lot of Army wives over many centuries. They found themselves competing with the families of the 1st Infantry Division, the "Big Red One," also stationed at Devens, for quarters in small towns around the Fort–Ayer, Harvard, Groton, Leominster, Pepperell, etc.

One incident that broke the monotony of training was related by Sgt. Ted Ramsland of C Troop. There always had been a rivalry between the Squadron A and Squadron C men. A plan was conceived to have a joint ride and "picnic" bivouac near Pepperell, New Hampshire intended to bring the two factions closer together. Things worked out well until late at night a few playful Squadron C troopers released the Squadron A horses off the picket lines resulting in a wild stampede. The good citizens of Ayer were startled out of their wits when late at night one hundred odd horses streamed pell-mell through their town bound for the home stables. After this the rivalry intensified and several NCO's lost their stripes.

In August the regiment engaged in a one-week field maneuver off the post with units of the 1st Division providing the opposition. The beautiful countryside and quaint villages of New England provided an incongruous setting for the practice of war. The natives were continually surprised at the appearance of armed men, horses and machines dashing back and forth across the landscape. In one instance, Captain Milton Kendall was leading his valiant motorcycle troopers into the sleepy town of Nashua only to find "enemy" forces already there. This led to a "fire fight" while the people on the streets and leaning out of windows looked on in astonishment. The rigors of field duty for Captain Bob Sweeney's horse troopers were eased by the appearance of a friendly milkman who delivered his products to their bivouac area every morning wherever they were.

These maneuvers gave the regiment an opportunity to work out many bugs in the new organization in preparation for a much larger field exercise soon to follow.

On 29 September 1941 the regiment left Fort Devens to participate in the First Army maneuvers in the Carolinas. For the first time as a horse-mechanized outfit, the 101st moved over the road in a single column. With its conglomeration of scout cars, motorcycles, tractor-trailers and various-sized trucks the column, moving in serials, extended several miles down the highways, while the daring young motorcycle troopers dashed up and down the column riding traffic control.

The horse troopers had a different thrill riding in the tractor-trailers as they barreled down the main highways on their first long trip. Each trailer held an entire eight-man squad with its horses, feed and equipment. The men rode in a small compartment in front separated from the horses only by removable "bay boards." Their main fear was that if the tractor-trailers had to slow down suddenly they would surely end up with several tons of horseflesh in their laps.

Upon arrival in North Carolina a tent camp was established in a field near the small town of Candor which would be used as a base camp for the next nine weeks. The only amenities in Candor were a small restaurant and a barbershop with two bathtubs where a customer could get a haircut and hot bath for two dollars.

At that time the press was calling the army the "Broomstick Army," because of the vast shortages of equipment throughout all units. Broomsticks represented machine guns, logs represented artillery pieces, trucks represented tanks, etc. The 101st Cavalry was particularly handicapped by a shortage of radios which prevented it from operating effectively in widely dispersed formations as it normally should. Motorcycles and scout cars were also in short supply.

As the maneuvers progressed it became clear to many that the inclusion of horse and mechanized units in one regiment was a mistake. Their capabilities were completely different and they did not complement each other in the completion of missions as the field manuals said they were meant to do. Furthermore, the use of tractor-trailers to move men and horses from one battle area to another was difficult. They were unwieldy and impossible to camouflage. In one instance the column commander was embarrassed in finding himself on a narrow-dead-end road. It took half a day to get the column turned around. In another situation the tractor-trailers became bogged down in a field after an all night rainstorm prevented them from being moved for almost an entire day. In spite of these problems the 101st Cavalry did a good job and was favorably mentioned in the critiques following each maneuver phase.

The regiment began its 800-mile march back to Fort Devens on 3 December, camped the last night out on the West Point plains and arrived at Devens on 6 December. Our only thought was that our year of active duty would be over in less than one month. This hope was, of course, exploded when news of Pearl Harbor was received the next day.

The outfit went back to its seemingly endless training on return to Devens but after Pearl Harbor things began to change. VI Corp, including the 101st Cavalry, had been earmarked for the Philippines in event of war with Japan but when those islands were overrun the plan was cancelled. In the meanwhile the U.S. Army Air Force began ferrying P-38 fighters to England using Dow Air Base at Bangor, Maine as the jump-off place. In January the regiment was ordered to provide security to the base and the Maine Coast in its vicinity.

The mechanized troops were dispatched to Bangor on a rotation basis and, as one can imagine, patrolling and out posting the wind and snow-blown airfield on foot and in open scout cars and motorcycles was not a choice assignment. After this the men found rest and relaxation and a chance to let off steam in Bangor, which was an old lumber town used to young loggers coming to the have fun.

On one Saturday night in particular the boys let off too much steam. That Sunday morning as F Troop C.O., I was summoned to the city jail where I found three very docile troopers. Upon inquiry it was revealed that two of them had tried to clean out Kerrigan's Bar defending the honor of a young lady customer who had been insulted. In another situation a young homesick private, at 1 a.m., had seen a telephone through the window of a Chinese laundry. He had to get in to make a phone call to his girl friend. The frightened proprietor who thought he was being robbed summoned the police. According to the first page newspaper account published, one patrolman was injured by the soldier's spurs while attempting to put him in the patrol wagon!

Back at Fort Devens the regiment began losing officers and N.C.O.'s in droves primarily to cadre newly formed units. Also, to their credit, dozens of the most experienced N.C.O.'s were ordered to Officers Training Schools after passing the necessary examinations. Then in late spring and summer several hundred draftees were received. Soon the regiment became a truly cosmopolitan outfit with New Yorkers, farmers, hillbillies, cowboys, mill workers, Indians and many other types.

Temporary units were established, staffed by regimental officers and NCO's to put the new men through basic training. During this period the regular troops could sometimes assemble less than thirty men at drill call. Under these conditions there was little chance of the regiment being called for overseas service. However, the regiment was proud of the fact that it had a higher percentage of NCO's going to OCS than perhaps any other unit in the Army.

In April 1942 another reorganization took place. This time the regiment became fully mechanized and was designated 101st Cavalry (Mecz.). The two squadrons became identical with three mechanized recon troops, F Troop (motorcycle) of the 2nd Squadron having been converted to a recon troop. At the same time the 101st began receiving jeeps to replace the motorcycles. This was a relief to many of those who had risked their lives riding them in the snow of New England and mud of the Carolinas.

It was a day of mixed emotions when the last horses left the regiment and were sent to the Army Remount Station at Front Royal, Virginia. As they paraded down the street past Regimental Headquarters it was lined with men, many with tears in their eyes. One sergeant expressed his feelings this way, "We had been proud of continuing in the old tradition but soon became envious of the mechanized boys who, at the end of the day, simply parked their vehicles and took off on pass or whatever while we had to unsaddle, groom, water and feed our horses and stow our gear. Our romance with horses was soon over. Anyway, who wants to go to war on such a noble animal?"

All the troopers wondered where their faithful mounts would end up. Some years later when I was a military advisor to Turkish Army

Units I got a big surprise. There on the picket lines of the First Turkish Cavalry Division stood dozens of the horses with the familiar Preston neck grand of the U.S. Army. Who knows how many of them may have been on the picket lines of the 101st Cavalry?

On 4 September the regiment left Fort Devens for Pine Camp (now Camp Drum) near Watertown, New York, for eight weeks of field training. By this time the outfit had almost fully recovered from its large personnel turnover and reorganization of the previous six months.

Pine Camp was a familiar stamping ground for the older troopers who had participated in summer training there for many years. The only apparent change was the substitution of motor parks for picket lines. The troopers who had been there before found that the movement of the vehicles, even jeeps, was greatly restricted compared to their experience with horses over the same terrain.

The 4th Armored Division was stationed there at the time and the 101st provided the "enemy" for its final training tests. During these tests many of us had the opportunity of seeing an entire tank battalion of the division with its fifty-odd medium tanks rapidly bearing down on us–a truly awesome sight not soon forgotten.

Toward the end of the training at Pine Camp a First Army team arrived to put the regiment through a training test. For reasons known only to them this test forced a dismounted attack on enemy fixed positions, one thing that mechanized cavalry is not trained, organized or equipped to do. Most of us felt that this was not a valid test of the regiment's capabilities.

On 26 October 1942 the 101st arrived back at Fort Devens from Pine Camp where training continued. For the last time would the men stand reveille at dawn in overcoats and long johns on the snow blown troop streets during a New England winter.

"Hurry up and Wait. Ft. Devens 1942."

"INTERIOR GUARD, FT. DEVENS 1941."

"Fording the Pee Dee. Carolina Maneuvers 1942."

"THE MAIN VEHICLE OF THE RECONNAISSANCE TROOPS WAS THE M8 ARMORED CAR."

SECTION 4

FORT MEADE AND THE EASTERN DEFENSE COMMAND

ON 10 March 1943 the regiment was transferred to Fort Mead, Maryland then headquarters of the Second U.S. Army. By this time it contained less than 45 percent of the officers and men who came into federal service with it. In the meanwhile several of the NCO's who went to OCS in 1941 came back as Second Lieutenants.

Upon arrival at Fort Meade the 101st became Mobile Reserve, Eastern Defense Command that had been established in 1942 to defend the coastline against submarine landed and parachute dropped saboteurs. It was a eerie sight at night to look out from the coast line and see the flash of explosions as torpedoes struck tankers only a few miles off the shoreline. Oil slicks from sinking ships polluted the coast from Maine to Florida.

In the meanwhile the war had heated up in Europe. The American invasion of Africa had already taken place the previous November and most of the troopers had become anxious to test their mettle in combat. They were not happy to have been diverted to the secondary, but important, mission of defending the coast while at the same time continuing the seemingly endless training.

While at Meade another First Army team descended on the regiment to conduct a training test. This test too became a frustrating experience. Using the main highway between Washington and New York as an axis of advance the regiment was required to "reconnoiter in zone" up through the center of Baltimore and other towns along the way all jam-packed with civilian traffic. The grand finale was an attack on fixed positions on the Fort Dix Military Reservation.

It was not long after this that Colonel Ackerman was relieved as Commanding Officer. He had been in the 101st Cavalry for many years and upon the death of Colonel James Howlett in 1938 had taken over the regiment. He was well liked and the rumor persisted that he had not been given a fair deal by the First Army.

On 20 August 1943 Colonel Charles B. McClelland, a young, aggressive officer, assumed command. "Mac" gave the outfit a shot in the arm. He made his mark early by emphasizing physical fitness for all officers and men. Wherever we went thereafter obstacle courses were built that would challenge the ability of an orangutan. Soon we were swinging on ropes with the greatest of ease across gullies 20 feet deep and climbing walls like monkeys.

In October 1943 the regiment was given the mission of guarding the Chesapeake Bay Sector of the Eastern Defense Command which extended from the eastern shore of Maryland to South Carolina. Regimental headquarters was established at Camp Ashby, Virginia, a former prisoner of war camp in back of Virginia Beach. 1st Squadron Headquarters was stationed at Camp Branch, North Carolina and the 2nd Squadron headquarters at Somerset, Maryland. This mission entailed the establishment of scattered lookout posts along the beaches and continuous patrolling in between them. Ironically, one stretch of coastline south of Virginia Beach had previously been patrolled by Coast Guard men mounted on horses but was now covered by ex-horse soldiers on foot.

The regiment had no sooner become well established in its new locations when it went through its third major reorganization–first from an all horse regiment to a horse-mechanized regiment, next to a completely mechanized regiment and this time to a Mechanized Cavalry Group organized as follows:

HQ and HQ Troop 101st Cavalry Group, Mecz.

HQ 101 Cavalry Recon Sq. Mecz.
   HQ & Service Troop
   Troops A, B & C (recon troops)
   Troop E (75 mm assault gun)
   Company F (light tank)

HQ 116 Cavalry Recon Sq. Mecz.
   HQ & Service Troop
   Troops A, B & C (recon troops)
   Troop E (75 mm assault gun)
   Company F (light tank)

In this configuration the two squadrons were only attached, not organic, to the group. By the addition of a headquarters and service troop they became administratively and logistically independent. The addition of an assault gun troop and a tank company made the squadrons more capable of independent action. The group headquarters had no administrative and service elements and retained only operational control of attached units.

In the new organization Colonel McClelland commanded this group with Lieutenant Colonel Leo Mortenson as executive officer. Lieutenant Colonel Milton Kendall commanded the 101st Cavalry Squadron with Major Henry Brock as executive officer. Lieutenant Colonel Hubert Leonard commanded the 116th Cavalry Squadron and Major Robert Feagin was his executive officer.

Soon after the reorganization was completed the squadrons began drawing the new M8 armored cars to replace the old and battered scout cars. On the present mission and scattered as they were, the units had little opportunity to train with these new vehicles and the tanks and assault guns they were receiving.

In January 1944 the 34th Cavalry Recon Squadron was attached to the group and the sector of responsibility was extended from Sandy Hook, New Jersey to a boundary south of Myrtle Beach, South Carolina. Putting it mildly this 850 mile coastline was a long stretch of territory for three cavalry squadrons to patrol.

Since this last reorganization was the way the group would finally go into combat it would be well to point out how the combat units were organized and something about their equipment.

The recon troops had three platoons, each consisting of an M8 armored car section with two armored cars, a scout section with four jeeps and a mortar section mounted in two jeeps. The platoon leader rode in a third armored car. The M8's carried one turret-mounted 17 mm cannon, one 30 caliber coaxial machine gun and one 30 caliber hull machine gun. Later a 50 caliber AA machine gun was mounted on a ring mount in the turret. The M8 was rated to withstand 50 caliber machine gun fire on the front and on the turret. The scout jeeps had pedestal-mounted 30 and 50 caliber machine guns. The mortar section carried one 60 mm mortar, later changed to 81 mm.

The assault gun troop consisted of three assault gun platoons, each containing two 75 mm Howitzers mounted on an armored track vehicle. This gun was intended for close support but could also be used for indirect fire at medium ranges.

The tank company had three platoons of five light M5 series tanks each. They carried the 37 mm turret gun with 30 caliber coaxial machine gun plus a 30 caliber hull machine gun and a 30 caliber AA machine gun was mounted on the turret. This tank was rated to withstand 20 mm cannon fire.

Although the Cavalry squadrons were not designed for "slugging matches" with enemy tanks and infantry, with their lightly armored vehicles and jeeps they were the fastest moving units in the Army with great flexibility due largely to their excellent radio communications.

SECTION 5

CAMP CAMPBELL, KENTUCKY
AND OVERSEAS MOVEMENT

ON 1 July 1944 the scattered units of the group were assembled and moved by rail to Camp Campbell for final training and preparation for overseas movement. Here were adequate firing ranges for the tank and assault gun weapons as well as small arms. The "camp followers" found makeshift homes in Clarksville, Tennessee and other small towns to be with their men for the last time. Forever?

On 26 October the group was moved to Camp Kilmer, New Jersey and five days later embarked at the Brooklyn Army Base bound for England on the transport *Argentina*, former luxury liner. Former passengers would have been amazed at the changes in this elegant ship, with most of the men sleeping in the hold on bunks stacked three and sometimes four deep. Good weather prevailed and they were permitted to walk the decks in shifts in order to avoid crowding.

SECTION 6

ENGLAND AND MOVEMENT TO FRANCE

ARRIVING at Liverpool, England on 12 November 1944 the Group was moved by rail to Camp Anty-Cross near Barrow-in-Furness in northern England close to the Scottish border. We were the first "Yanks" to be stationed there. It had been used by a Scottish Highland brigade which had just gone to France.

After the several days quarantine required by the British on all troops coming into England, the troopers were given their first passes to go out on the town. The next morning unusual stories were circulated about the terrific hospitality of the British lassies. It must be remembered that most of the young British men had been away at the war for several years. Some of the young ladies gave our boys the answer to the age-old question of "What do the Scots wear under their kilts?"

Again the group was held up getting into the active fighting because the ships containing all the vehicles and heavy equipment were delayed for a month in reaching England. Without it time was spent on long road marches across the beautiful English countryside and on other dismounted training.

When equipment began arriving the supply and maintenance men did yeoman's work putting it into service and making several modifications. Upright iron T-bars were installed on the front of the jeeps to counter a nasty German habit of stretching wire neck-high across roads. The M8 armored cars and other vehicles were provided with 50 caliber AA machine guns on ring mounts.

In the meanwhile the deep British sense of hospitality reached out in genuine welcome to the equally friendly and well-behaved "Yanks."

Barrow-in-Furness and Camp Anty-Cross and the good people there will always hold a warm place in the hearts of the men of the 101st. Christmas Eve midnight services and the mess hall afterwards with hot coffee and doughnuts and the British Red Cross girls who made them added to these memories. Here we heard Bing Crosby sing "White Christmas" for the first time over BBC.

On 4 January 1945 the 101st moved by rail and road to Camp Barton-Stacey in southern England to prepare for movement to France. General-purpose vehicles were drawn and serviced and combat loads were issued from ordnance depots. On 29 January the group moved to the South Hampton marshaling area and embarked on four LSTs, two Liberty ships and a troop transport.

The LSTs and troop ships arrived at Le Havre, France 31 January while the two Liberty ships containing the reconnaissance troops disembarked up the Seine River at Rouen. From there the units assembled at Camp Twenty Grand near Duclair, France where orders were received to move to the Faulequemont area behind the battle line south of the Saar River in the Seventh Army sector. As the columns moved eastward closer to the fighting all of us were thinking of how we would react in battle for the first time. While passing through Soissons and Verdun our thoughts also dwelt on the terrible carnage inflicted during the stalemated battles in that area during World War I. The units closed in bivouac at St. Avold, France on 7 February.

SECTION 7

SITUATION ON THE WESTERN FRONT – FEBRUARY 1945

FOLLOWING the rapid withdrawal of German troops across France late in the summer of 1944 they had turned and made a stand on or close to the French-German border. At that time the American supply lines had been badly over-extended to the point where the units were forced to stop to wait for supplies and replacements. Efforts to continue offensive operations were further delayed by the Battle of the Bulge since all major effort had to be directed toward reducing the large salient punched into the Allied lines by the German army.

It was not until February 1945 that General Eisenhower directed that the attack be resumed on a wide front from the North Sea to the Swiss border. The Seventh Army was then occupying the line of the Saar River with the Third Army on its left blank and the French First Army on the right. Its first task was to cross the Saar River and breech the Siegfried Line. It was at this point that the 101st Cavalry went into the line.

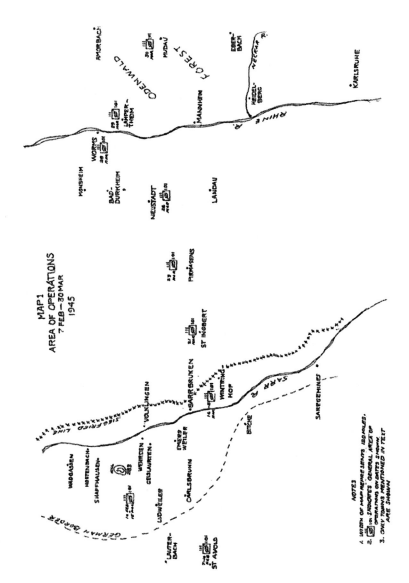

SECTION 8

FIGHTING ON THE LINE OF THE SAAR RIVER

AT St. Avold on 10 February the 101st was attached to XV Corps, Seventh Army, Sixth Army Group under General Jacob Devers, with orders to relieve the 106th Cavalry Group in its defensive mission along the line Emmersweiler - Wadgassen, German. The group headquarters and that of the 116th Recon Squadron were set up at Lauterbach two miles from the German border. The 101st Recon Squadron set up its CP at Carlsbrunn, German.

When the group relieved the 106th Cavalry on 11 February it inherited a small army at the same time. Attached were the following units:

17th Field Artillery Group
   93rd Armored Field Artillery Battalion
   802nd Field Artillery Battalion
1185th Engineer Group (Combat)
   48th Engineer Battalion (C)
   165th Engineer Battalion (C)
   2756th Engineer Battalion (C)
2nd Chemical Mortar Battalion (4.2 mm)
Air Support Party
IPW Team
Allied Military Government Detachment
Counter-Intelligence Detachment

In the execution of the group defensive mission the engineers not only provided their usual engineer support but fought as infantry which was most welcome to a cavalry unit which was devoid of an organic dismounted infantry capability. The 4.2 mortars of the mortar battalion provided extremely lethal close-fire support in addition to that of the attached artillery battalions which could call in additional medium and heavy artillery when needed.

Within days of taking over from the 106th Cavalry Group, orders were received from XV Corps to prepare for an attack to close on the

Saar River preparatory to crossing operations. The date of this attack was contingent upon the progress of other corps units. In the meanwhile the defensive line was occupied by the establishment of strong points joined by foot and vehicular patrols. The bulk of the two squadrons was held back in mobile reserve. This defense line had been established back in the previous November and it was thickly strewn with anti-personnel and anti-tank mines which had not been recorded, making it extremely dangerous to move throughout the area.

Combat operations consisted primarily of aggressive patrolling by both sides and the exchange of mortar and artillery fire. One matter of interest occurred when one of our patrols discovered one of Hitler's "Baby Factories." In order to improve the Aryan race he had set up resort-like establishments occupied by blonde, blue-eyed, healthy maidens who were willing to sacrifice their virginity to selected, equally blonde, blue-eyed and healthy young German soldiers who were given one week's leave to fulfill this additional duty to the Fatherland. Many men volunteered for patrol duty in this area thereafter!

On 12 March orders were received to execute the attack which had been delayed by strong enemy resistance given the 70th Infantry Division on the group's right flank. The night of 13 March our combat patrols gained detailed information of the enemy positions. Using this information the main attack took off the following morning supported by close air support and artillery and led by dismounted troopers.

The 101st Cavalry Squadron met particularly hard resistance from an enemy strong point on Hill 283 overlooking the entire battle area. Captain Ralph Ritchie, leading A Troop up the hill, was wounded three times before being evacuated in the desperate fighting on the slopes. Lieutenant Robert Ulmschneider took over the troop and remained in command until the end of the war.

All of the recon troops reinforced with tank and assault gun platoons took part in this fight. Captain Abe Friedman's B Troop of the 101st attacked along the flank of A Troop. C. Troop of the 101st, Captain Biels commanding, attacked down the Ludweiler - Geislautern road and cleared the latter town. Lieutenant Borkowski led a platoon, sometimes on hands and knees, through dense mines and booby traps, entered the town of Schaffhausen and extended his patrol to Hostenbach. A Troop, commanded by Captain Al Burgess and B Troop of the 116th commanded by Captain Gus Littleton soon followed, mopping up those two towns and continued the attack to the river. C. Troop of the 116th commanded by Captain Lou Bossert attached to the 101st Recon Squadron got in a heavy fight for the Wehrden - Volklingen Bridge faced with fire from across the river.

By sundown of the 15th the group had taken all strong points and towns on the west side of the Saar at the expense of 33 killed, wounded and missing. Lieutenant Colonel Leonard, CO of the 116th was wounded and evacuated in this fight but was returned to duty one month later. The men of the 101st Cavalry had met their baptism of fire and performed like veterans.

On the morning of 16 March the group, now assigned to XXI Corps, was attached to the 63rd Infantry Division and directed to assemble in the vicinity of Hellimer, France after relief on the Saar River line by the 70th Infantry Division. All units previously attached were detached and one company of the 253rd Infantry, the 93rd AFA Battalion and the reconnaissance troop of the 63rd Division were attached. Soon thereafter all officers and platoon sergeants were killed or wounded by a mortar attack. Captain Howard Bissland, 101st Cavalry liaison officer, was placed in command.

At this time the 63rd Division was east of the SAAR, just south of Saarbrucken, preparing a final assault on the Siegfried Line. The group was put into the front facing the Siegfried Line between Gudingen and Ensheim and directed to begin aggressive patrolling to probe for weak spots.

The Siegfried Line contained a combination of "Dragon's Teeth," anti-tank ditches, pill boxes and mine fields. It had excellent fields of fire from commanding positions and any daytime movement of our troops was immediately met with small arms, mortar and artillery fire. An order signed by the Fuhrer himself found on a captured German read in part as follows, "Any man who is captured without being wounded or having fought to the last will be disgraced and his family cut off from all support." It appeared from this that the Germans were not about to give up this line easily.

The men of the 101st looked on in awe as the initial assault on the line was begun by the 253rd Infantry Regiment on our right. Made up into assault teams of infantry, engineers, tanks and tank-dozers which closely followed a curtain of fire laid down by smoke and high explosive artillery shells, they methodically worked through the line section by section blasting "Dragon's Teeth," demolishing pill boxes and filling anti-tank ditches. The relentless attack continued through the night illuminated by eerie "artificial moonlight" created by bouncing searchlight beams off the low flying clouds. We thanked God that we had not been chosen for this task, and the same time our admiration for the infantry and engineers increased hundredfold.

By the second day a narrow breech was made through the line and the 101st was directed to exploit this breach. At the same time our patrols reported that German troops were withdrawing on both sides of the breakthrough to avoid encirclement. Troop A, 116th Cavalry, reinforced, was selected to make the initial passage through the line and to seize the town of St. Ingbert four miles to the rear and to block all roads into the area. The remainder of the group followed with orders to protect the 63rd Division's flanks as it completed the breakthrough.

This was the first penetration of the Siegfried Line on the Seventh Army front and therein lies an interesting anecdote. We had an acting public relations officer, name best withheld, who sometimes overdid the glorification of the 101st. He wrote a press release for Stars and Stripes headed, "101st Cavalry first to break Siegfried Line in 7th Army." Upon reading this the commanding general of the 63rd Infantry Division blew his top and immediately called group headquarters. The recipient of the call explained later that "he chewed my ass for five minutes without stopping." This was understandable since his division had lost many good men fighting through the line. We had passed through after most of the heavy fighting was over.

SECTION 9

ADVANCE TO THE RHINE BRIDGEHEAD

ON 21 March, the 101st was relieved from attachment to the 63rd Infantry Division and came under direct control of XXI Corps with orders to assemble near Bitche, France.

Troop A 101st Squadron, Lieutenant Robert Ulmschneider commanding, was placed in detached service with HQ Sixth Army Group for a special mission.

From this time on the 101st would enter a war of movement and an environment for which lightly equipped, but highly mobile cavalry was designed. The squadron commanders elected to organize troop- and platoon-sized task forces made up of reconnaissance, tank and assault gun elements. Where we were fortunate to have medium tanks or tank destroyers attached they too were farmed out to the other lower units. The task forces normally operated out of supporting distance of each other, but excellent radio contact provided coordination of movement except when they ended up at night behind German forward elements and had to exercise radio silence.

At this time information from prisoners indicated that the German Army planned to fight a delaying action to the east side of the Rhine River 60 miles away and there make a determined stand. In the meanwhile the rest of XXI Corps had passed through the Siegfried Line and was in pursuit of the Germans. The 101st was ordered to follow along and mop up all resistance in the Corps zone which was then 20 miles wide. This was done against German delaying forces blocking the narrow roads in the beautiful Harz Mountains. Abandoned supply dumps, ammunition stores, weapons and hospitals were found and reported to XXI Corps.

The group headquarters entered Pirmasens late the afternoon of the 23rd and here at close range saw the devastating affects of allied aerial bombing. The town of perhaps 50,000 was practically leveled. German families were huddled together wherever they could find shelter. Others wandered in a daze through still smoking rubble. Broken water mains spouted water and the smell of death was everywhere. That night the group found a place to bivouac near a cemetery at the edge of town. In back of the buildings were row upon row of coffins of the unburied dead. We were glad to soon move on.

The following day the results of allied air power could be seen again along a mountain road. For well over a mile were at least 200 dead horses from a German supply column that had been strafed, still harnessed to their wrecked wagons. I for one was not ashamed to feel the same deep sorrow and anguish that I had felt on seeing our dead GIs and, for that matter, the young teenage dead German soldiers.

On 28 March the group arrived at its first objective line, Landau - Neustadt, which abruptly divides the mountains from the flat, fertile valley of the Rhine Valley. At that time XV Corps on the XXI Corps left flank was in process of forcing a crossing of the Rhine at the ancient city of Worms 30 miles to the north. XXI Corps was ordered to turn north to this area on the axis Neustadt - Bad Durkheim - Worms. The 101st Cavalry was ordered to protect the corps' line of communications, mop up enemy resistance, control movement of civilian traffic and divert or transport all non-German POWs and DPs (displaced persons) to POW and DP centers established by the corps. Considering the size of the corps zone of advance this was a large order.

After the rapid retreat of the Germans the countryside was filled with hundreds of POWs of every Allied nationality, including Americans. Added to these were DPs (Displaced Persons) from every country overrun by the German Army - Poles, Ukrainians, Lithuanians, French, Italians, etc. They had been brought to Germany as slave labor and forced to live in DP compounds under miserable conditions. These people had existed by looting after breaking out of the camps abandoned by the retreating Germans. This situation continued throughout Germany until the end of the war and for weeks thereafter. Later on one of our troops "adopted" an Italian cook and toward war's end group headquarters "adopted" two comely Ukranian sisters as maids with a strict understanding among us that there would be no "hanky-panky."

Many small German units were caught as they moved over secondary roads to the west toward the river hoping somehow to get across. During the operation over 60 German prisoners were taken and many casualties inflicted wherever they had established delaying positions that had to be destroyed. From the actions of the German Army at this point we began to feel that victory was just around the corner but, as later events proved, we were in for a rude awakening.

On 29 March the group passed through other corps' units at Worms and cross the Rhine on a pontoon bridge screened by smoke and went into an assembly area at Lampertheim two miles east of the river.

At Lampertheim orders were received to secure the Seventh Army bridgehead line in the corps sector 30 miles to the east on a line Eberbach - Mudau - Amorbach. This mission would take us through the steeply wooded slopes and narrow valleys of the beautiful Odenwalk Forest legendary in German folklore.

In order to uncover and drive back enemy forces in the forest, the squadrons broke into a total of six task forces while group headquarters itself reinforced with tank and assault gun platoons formed a seventh. In some instances the troops further broke down into platoon-size task forces to cover all roads. The extremely rugged terrain forced all columns to operate exclusively in the narrow valleys.

This terrain was ideally suited for delaying actions which the Germans used to the utmost by means of road blocks, destroyed bridges, mines and other obstacles. Here for the first time our columns were subjected to strafing by enemy aircraft as the German defense began to slowly tighten up.

The Neckar River ran along the south flank of the XXI Corps zone and the city of Heidelberg, because of its long cultural history, had been declared an "open city" by the Allied and German high commands. This meant it was exempt from shelling and occupation by either side. Heidelberg lay on the south bank of the Neckar and one of our columns proceeding up the north shore of the river became engaged in intense fire fight with the defenders of a road block directly across from the city. As one trooper later described it, it was "weird" feeling to be fighting like mad across the narrow river while hundreds of men, women and children lined the banks and rooftops to watch as though they were seeing a Saturday afternoon sports event!

Our units reached the designated bridgehead line by evening of 30 March. At this point the 101st had moved almost 100 miles in eight days with varying degrees of opposition. The surprise was yet to come.

SECTION 10

BATTLES ALONG THE TAUBER RIVER

PRIOR to nightfall of 30 March elements of the 4th Infantry Division relieved the 101st Cavalry of defending the bridgehead line and it was directed to continue the advance to the line Hochstadt - Neustadt - Rothenberg some 55 miles to the east.

The composition of XXI Corps had changed since leaving the Rhine. The 63rd, 70th and 71st Infantry divisions had been replaced by the 4th and 42nd Infantry Divisions and the 12th Armored Division. Troop A 101st Cavalry Recon Squadron still remained with HQ. Sixth Army Group.

As the Group approached the valley of the Tauber River the forward elements began to meet ever increasing enemy resistance. Enemy air became more active and here for the first time we were attacked by Luftwaffe jet fighters. Hitler had expected to turn the tide of war with these jets but as a result of Allied bombing of factories and a shortage of trained pilots they reached the battlefields too late and too few. Fortunately for the Allies, the untrained pilots usually overshot their targets because of the higher speed of these aircraft. Here also, for the first time, we encountered the famous "Nebelwerfers," which consisted of up to 48 6.2 mm rockets mounted on tanks or trucks that could be fired simultaneously or in tandem with devastating effects.

By nightfall of 31 March the 116th Recon Squadron had reached the Tauber River at Tauberbishopfsheim on the north; however, the 101st Recon Squadron had been held up by extremely heavy resistance on the south and had gotten only as far as Eubigheim, ten miles from the river.

At first light on Easter Sunday the advance continued, but at a much slower pace; however, A Troop of the 116th sideslipped the enemy at Tauberbishopfsheim and cross the river. On the south the 101st Recon Squadron was stopped cold at Bad Mergentheim by defenders on the east side of the river. In the center, group headquarters reinforced with tanks and assault guns attempting to

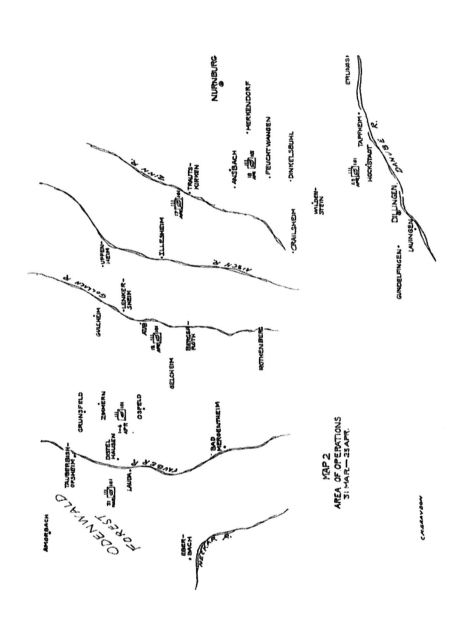

move through Lauda was stopped by heavy fire from the east side of the river.

Here, but for the grace of God and Captain Walter Kohnle, Assistant S-3, the entire group operations and intelligence sections in a half-track would have been wiped out. The column was held up by fire on the main street and when Captain Kohnle jokingly mentioned that according to the field manuals we should disperse the vehicles, we took his advice and backed into a side street. Not more than a minute later we could hear the characteristic "gobble, gobble" of Nebelwerfers as they came down and struck the street exactly where the half-track had been. Nothing but a large hole in the street was left! After the German forces were routed from the high ground east of the river by tank and assault gunfire the column crossed.

In the past two days the group had lost two of its young liaison officers and one NCO. In two separate incidents, Lieutenants George Langdon and George Gardner were killed by sniper fire and in a third incident T-4 William Kornblu, radio operator with another liaison party, was killed. These men were extremely vulnerable to ambush when they visited units so widely separated in hostile country. As of 1 April the group had suffered a total of 93 killed, wounded and missing.

In the last few days of action the group had determined the contour of a heavily defended MLR (main line of resistance) in the corps sector on the line Bad Mergentheim - Osfeld - Simmern - Grunfeld on the east side of the Tauber. The night of 1 April the group was attached to the 4th Infantry Division and given orders to screen the division front and south flank as it closed on the river. Most of the group task forces were already on the designated screening line so there was a temporary respite in the fighting except in the center where Captain Louis Bossert's C Troop of the 116th ran into a hornet's nest at the little town of Osfeld when it attempted to penetrate the enemy MLR. Entering the outskirts the troop met small arms, panzer faust, mortar and Nebelwerfer fire and was forced to withdraw. A combat team of the 4th Division coming up on the right flank was also turned back. On the following day C Troop again fought its way into Osfeld but was again forced out and the infantry on its flank could make no progress.

On 4 April the commanding general of the 4th Division ordered a coordinated attack all along the line using two combat teams and the 116th Cavalry. C Troop again attacked its nemesis, Osfeld. The attack continued through the 4th, 5th and 6th of April when it was finally successful and the MLR was broken.

On 8 April the group was attached to the 12th Armored Division and was directed to exploit the breakthrough and conduct a reconnaissance in force to a stop line some 30 miles to the southeast. Troop C of the 101st was attached back to the 4th Division, leaving the squadron with only one reconnaissance troop.

SECTION 11

ADVANCE TO THE DANUBE

THE Germans had not given up the fight by any means and it was now a race to prevent them from establishing another MLR. Practically every one of the dozens of towns in the zone of advance had to be fought for against the stubborn Germans who frequently counterattacked with tanks and assault guns. Resistance was particularly strong along the lines of the Gollach, the Aisch and the Zinn Rivers.

The thin-skinned light tanks and armored cars of the 101st Cavalry were completely vulnerable to the tank guns of the Wehrmacht and the 37 mm guns on our vehicles could not penetrate the thick plate on them. However, our fast-moving cavalry forces out ahead would locate the enemy and, if they could, overcome the resistance. If not, the heavier and more powerful 12th Armored Division Combat Commands' medium tanks and armored infantry would be called up to do the job.

On the night of 17 April advance units of the group had closed on the Zinn River in the vicinity of Troutskirchen. Since the fighting around Osfeld, these pitched battles had continued day and night over a zone 20 miles wide and over 35 miles long. Troopers who were there will long remember such towns as Gulchheim, Baldersheim, Uffenheim, Gulchheim, Aub and Bergeroth where some of the sharpest fighting took place. It became standard procedure when entering each town to summon the burgermeister and give him the rules of martial law that would be enforced and have him direct all citizens to turn in their weapons and cameras for confiscation. If the unit was to remain overnight the burgermeister was told to arrange for billets in private homes, gasthauses, chateaus or whatever was available.

The reaction of the German people varied considerably from a sullen attitude to one of friendliness (whether genuine or not). Rarely was there outright belligerence. Most were glad that the Americans and not the Russians had come. No one would admit to being a Nazi, although it was well-known that all the cities and towns were run by them.

For some time we had been witnessing the disintegration of not only the Wehrmacht but of an entire nation as the Allies closed in on the German heartland from both directions. Hitler's divisions, with few exceptions, were down to less than one-third strength. Added to their ranks had been thousands of school-age young boys and old men unfit for battle. Factories had been destroyed and supply lines repeatedly cut. Many of us held a grudging respect for the way they continued to resist with as much skill as they did. It was apparent, however, that they were losing their will to resist with the exception of Hitler's own SS Troops who continued to fight fanatically.

By now all Germans must have realized that the war was lost except for Adolph Hitler, who still had dreams of glory for himself and his country. Information had been developing from Allied Intelligence Services that he was planning to build up a fortress of final resistance high in the Bavarian Alps. There he would hold off the Allied armies until he could come to favorable terms with Eisenhower and the Russians. This fortress was referred to as "National Redoubt." To meet this contingency XXI Corps was directed to move forces as rapidly as possible into the Alps to prevent the building up. Consequently, early the morning of 18 April Headquarters 12th Armored Division ordered a change in the direction of advance from southeast to south - a change of 90 degrees. The next axis of advance was to be Ansbach - Fechtwangen - Crailsheim.

In the meanwhile the composition of the group was changed. The 101st Recon Squadron was attached to the 4th Infantry Division and the 92nd Recon Squadron of the 12th Armored Division was attached to the group. The 342nd AFA Battalion was also attached.

At 0700, 18 April, CCA followed by CCB of the 12th Armored moved southwest on the new axis while the 101st Cavalry moved parallel to them to protect the open southeast flank of the column. Although enemy resistance had weakened in the past two days this new mission did not turn out to be a "piece of cake." It was obvious that the Germans were engaged in a delaying action but they were not giving up ground without a stubborn fight. The 92nd Recon Squadron immediately ran into one strongly held roadblock after another. Troop A of the 116th Recon Squadron followed by Troop C moving parallel to the 92nd on its south flank got as far as Wolfram - Eschenbach and ran into a determined fight for the town. Troop C bypassed that town and attacked Merkendorf one-half mile down the road and after a prolonged fight entered the town, driving elements of the SS 17th Panzer Grenadier Division to the southwest where it dug in a short distance away.

Before daylight on 19 April the SS Troops counterattacked C Troop which had the First Platoon of F Troop and Third Platoon of E Troop attached. The attack came from three directions overwhelming the outposts and entering the town. Captain Bossert's after-action report best portrays what happened:

> "The Troop CP was attacked by panzer faust fire and four SS Troopers were killed as they attempted to enter the windows. Under the circumstances, organization for battle was impossible. For over two hours a series of bloody hand-to-hand battles were fought throughout the town. Attackers were repelled by small arms, knives and furniture thrown from the windows. At daylight enemy reinforcements were seen approaching from the west. Machine gun and small arms fire was brought to bear upon the enemy and the attack was broken up before it reached the town. By this time the situation in town was under control. Eighty SS Troopers were killed 16 captured and an undetermined number were wounded. Troop C and attached units suffered (only) 19 casualties!"

For this action, the action at Osfeld and others, C Troop was awarded the Presidential Unit Citation.

After two months of hard, successful fighting with surprisingly few casualties the long, arduous training back in the United States was paying off hundredfold. The men of the 101st were fighting with the skill of hardened veterans; furthermore, the commanders from the "Old Man" on down were using excellent judgment in successfully accomplishing their assigned missions without needlessly losing men. The type of scattered, small unit actions we were in engaged in continually tested the leadership of officers and non-coms at all levels of command.

The night of 18-19 April XXI Corps again changed the direction of the 12th Armored Division attack to due south from the town of Fechtwangen. At the same time the 101st Recon Squadron reverted to group control from attachment to the 4th Infantry Division. The group was relieved of its blocking mission and directed to reconnoiter south in front of the combat commands. The resistance was becoming extremely "spotty." In some places roadblocks were left undefended while in others delaying positions were defended with the utmost determination, usually by SS troops.

Troop C of the 101st Recon Squadron operating on the right flank ran into trouble at the small town of Schoffloch and could not break through. The medium tanks and Armored Infantry of CCA were brought up and overran the enemy defense. Soon thereafter the squadron was unable to penetrate the defenses at Wildenstein; however, C Troop sideslipped the town and came up on the German rear. Lieutenant Colonel Kendall formed Task Force Brock (Major Henry Brock, Sq. Ex. O) consisting of his B Troop and B Troop of the 116th drawn from Group reserve. After a prolonged three-hour attack coming from both directions the resistance was broken.

By now forward units of the 12th Armored and the 101st were approximately 60 miles from the Danube River. It had become clear from intelligence sources that the German plan was to leave strong delaying forces north of the river while building up well-placed defensive positions south of it with the main forces. It was anticipated that the bridges over the river would be prepared for demolition and, under the circumstances, speed was of the essence. If resistence held up the advance it would be bypassed where possible.

At 2300, 21 April the division ordered an advance on a broad front to secure the bridges in its area of operations. CCA was directed to secure bridges in the Dillingen area, CCB the bridges at Hochstadt and the 101st Recon Squadron was assigned the bridges in the vicinity of Lauingen and Tapfheim. The group commander ordered the 92nd to capture bridges in the vicinity of Erlingshoffen while the 116th was assigned the mission of mopping up bypassed Germans.

The 101st Recon Squadron moved early 22 April, made a bold night march and, with the assistance of CCA, cleared the town of Laucheim and continued on only to have the two bridges at Lauingen destroyed minutes before it arrived. The 92nd moved before dawn on the 23rd and as its forward units drew closer to the river the German rear guard fought them off until their main forces had crossed the river. The blasts of the bridge being blown at Erlinhoffen could be heard two miles away. In the meanwhile CCA entered Dillingen and with complete surprise captured the main bridge intact while at the same time the 101st Recon Squadron fought off a strong German counterattack in the vicinity of Lauingen on the Division's right flank.

MAP 3
AREA OF OPERATIONS
24 APR – 8 MAY 1945

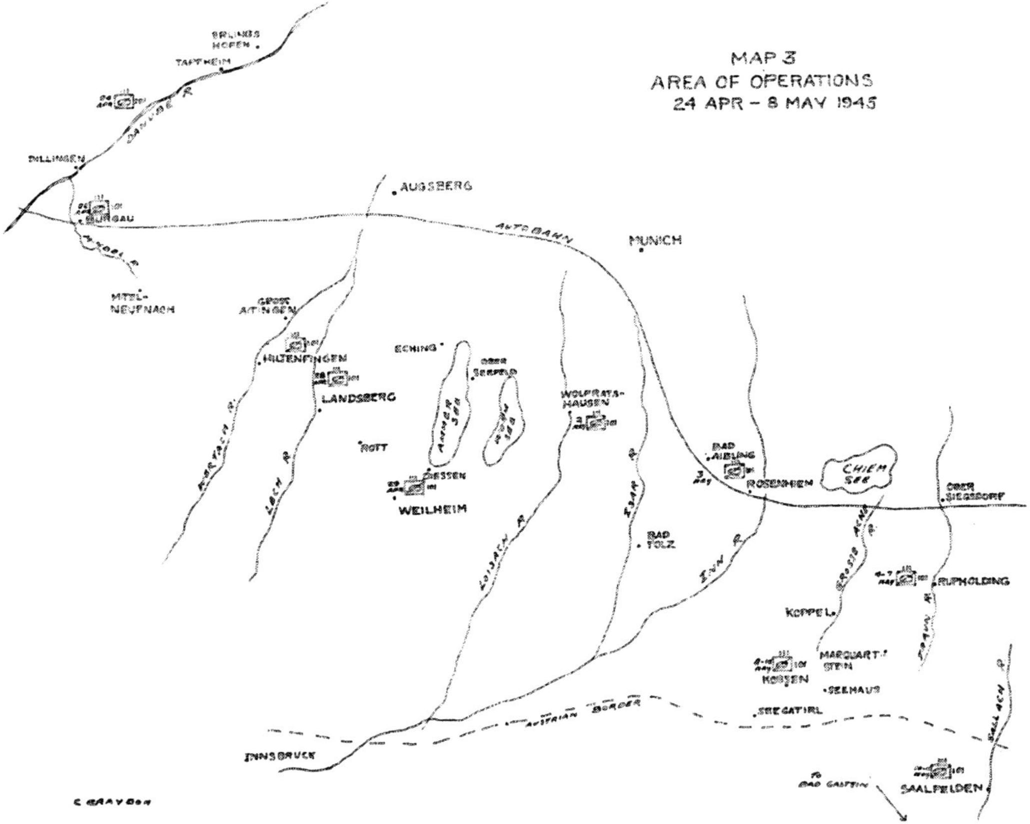

SECTION 12

FROM THE DANUBE TO THE ALPS

AFTER searching for additional crossings over the Danube in conjunction with CCB and CCR, the 101st was directed to move south, seize the bridges across the Mindel River five miles away and continue a reconnaissance in force to the southeast. On 24 April the 2nd Recon Squadron headed for Burgau, where the Frankfurt - Salzburg autobahn crosses the Mindel, and seized the bridges there. A strong counter attack was held off the night of 25 April.

The 116th coming up parallel to the 92nd also hit resistance near the autobahn and, at the same time, made a remarkable discovery. Hidden in a large, wooded area were several hundred jet aircraft in various stages of completion! They had undoubtedly been moved from aircraft factories in the vicinity of Munich to avoid Allied bombing.

The 101st Recon Squadron moving to the left of the 116th encountered dug-in enemy defenses supported by the dreaded 88 mm AA guns used effectively as AT guns. At the same time the 63rd Infantry Division on the right flank of the 12th Armored Division was fighting off a day-long German counterattack. It was apparent that the Germans were building up another main line of resistance along the general line of the autobahn.

The afternoon of 26 April an event of considerable importance occurred. An officer courier from the 17th SS Corps was intercepted with classified documents and a marked map showing the German dispositions and plans for a coordinated counterattack to be made by three divisions. This map was brought to Group headquarters where it was noticed that the corps' left boundary along the Mindel River was not clearly defined. On a chance that this boundary might not be strongly defended, the 92nd was directed to make its main effort down the river valley. This hunch paid off when the 92nd broke through with relative ease. The 116th followed the 92nd and soon both squadrons were operating in the rear of the German defense. With direct pressure from the 101st Recon Squadron on the left, the enemy defenses in the 12th Armored Division zone-of-attack soon collapsed.

(The entire maneuver was later used by the Tactics Division of the Armored School, Fort Knox, as a classic example of cavalry action.)

There was still to be no respite in the fighting when on 26 April Colonel McClelland ordered the 92nd to proceed without delay to seize bridges over the Wertach River 20 miles to the south at Hiltenfingen while the 116th moved through and secured the approaches from the south. The 101st was forced to fight all the way but finally captured the bridge at Gross Aitengen. While the 101st was fight off counterattacks the 92nd and 116th were ordered to continue on to the Lech River 10 miles to the southeast and capture the bridges in the vicinity of Landsberg. Both squadrons reached the Lech in record time only to have all bridges along the river blown up in their faces. The three squadrons spent the remainder of 17 April reconnoitering the river for crossing sites and reporting those destroyed bridges which could be most easily repaired.

During the wet, cold weather of late winter and spring most of our troopers could find some kind of cover at night - commandeered private homes, farm houses, barns, gasthauses and even schlosses (castles). Only recently Colonel McClelland reminded me of an interesting experience in this regard. The group headquarters moved into Hiltenfingen about 1 a.m. the night of 27 April. The search for quarters resulted in a particularly unsavory gasthaus for the staff. Colonel McClelland was awakened before dawn by Major Leo Nawn, Group S-2 to read a message from 12th Armored Division and when doing so asked the colonel who his roommate was. Unbeknownst to "Mace" a dead German was under his bed!

The orders that came in indicated the assembly of large concentrations of German troops in the general area of Munich 20 miles to the northeast. The division was directed to cross the Lech that same morning, seize and hold Wilhelm, Pensburg and Bad Tolz to the south and block passes into the Bavarian Alps. The group was directed to have one squadron move in advance of CCA to capture the above towns and the group was directed to screen the long, exposed left flank of the division as it bypassed Munich. This maneuver was undoubtedly intended to prevent the Germans from reinforcing Hitler's dream of "National Redoubt" with forces assembling near Munich.

The 12th Armored engineers worked feverishly all night to repair a railroad bridge at Landsberg as the only feasible crossing site. The group was ordered to make the initial crossing and, accordingly, headed for the bridge as rapidly as possible. Before reaching it many of us got the shock of our lives.

In the early dawn wraith-like figures could be seen wandering aimlessly along the roads and through the fields. They turned out to be hollow-eyed, living skeletons wearing striped pajama-like garments hanging from their protruding bones. Up ahead heavy, dark smoke arose above a tree line and behind it we came upon one of Hitler's notorious concentration camps. Inside was pure horror.

Upon learning of the approach of American troops, the prisoners had broken through the barbed wire, killed the German guards and were in the process of looting and looking for food in the nearby countryside. The gas chambers and burning ovens were still filled with bodies. Dead and dying prisoners and guards alike lay strewn throughout the compound. Two miles farther on was a stalled railroad train with a string of cattle cars filled with dead prisoners. Evidence indicated that they had been machine gunned down while in the cars. No one will ever know why the fiends were trying to move these poor wretches only to kill them somewhere else. Memories of those sights will never be forgotten by anyone who saw them.

At 0600 units of the group began cross the railroad bridge at Landsberg in the order of the 116th Recon Squadron, the 101st Recon Squadron, Group Headquarters and the 92nd Recon Squadron. The division began crossing in the afternoon with CCA leading. The use of only one bridge demanded that units cross on a tight time schedule. Group Headquarters spent an embarrassing 15 minutes stalled on the bridge by one of the "liberated" German vehicles which had broken down in the middle. It finally had to be dumped unceremoniously into the river.

Upon crossing the Lech the squadrons, without stopping, fanned out and streamed to the southwest on their newly assigned missions. The 116th followed by CCA headed for Weilheim and Bad Tolz. The 101st followed by the 92nd aimed for the bridges to the north of Ammer See and Wurm See. The rat race was on again!

The 116th got as far as Rott halfway to Weilheim before it was stopped by defenders inside that walled town. After an intense battle, B Troop was left to maintain contact with the enemy while A and C Troops bypassed during the night. By morning of 29 April they had captured the bridges over the Amper River at the foot of Ammer See vicinity of Diesson. By noon B Troop broke through the defenses at Rott and cleared Weilheim, followed by CCA one-half hour later.

The 101st Recon Squadron came within a few miles of its first objective, the bridge across the Amper River just north of Ammer See, only to be stopped by demolitions all along the only access road. This required a wide detour to the south but within a few miles the leading task force was again stopped by an attacking force of infantry supported by several Tiger tanks equipped with 88 mm guns. The resulting battle ended when the squadron supported by fire from the 342nd Armored Field Artillery Battalion forced the Germans to withdraw. The artillery battalion C.O. had long since given up attempting to cover the entire front of the far ranging and fast moving 101st Cavalry columns from one position. Accordingly, he had farmed out his three batteries to the three squadrons.

After this fight the squadron turned north again and got in a position to prevent the Germans from repairing and crossing the partially destroyed bridge at the north end of Ammer See. In the meanwhile the 116th had been given a new mission to precede CCA, move through the mountain passes in the Alps and capture Innsbruck some 70 miles to the south. The 101st was directed to move to the south end of Ammer See to take over the 116th blocking mission while the 92nd moved up from reserve to take over the mission of the 101st. Somewhat like a game of musical chairs!

In the midst of all this movement, in the afternoon of 29 April, two representatives of an anti-Nazi group in Munich appeared at the Group Cp IN Diessen and reported that Nazi authority in the city had been overthrown. They requested that American troops enter it right away and restore order. They promised that there would be no German resistance. Accordingly, Colonel McClelland ordered the 101st Recon Squadron to move into Munich. Half-way there however, the squadron was met with withering fire from Ober - Seefeld while a strong enemy force could be seen attempting to outflank it. It was apparent that the information about taking Munich without opposition was false so the mission was cancelled. Lieutenant Colonel Kendall, squadron C.O., stated later that he was mighty glad he didn't have to try to capture a city of over one million people with his 800 men.

Jack Langridge, group operations sergeant, while posting the situation map the night of 30 April, showing our units and those of the Germans going in all directions, remarked that it looked like the "damndest can of worms" he had ever seen. And it was just that. The German Army was in a state of complete disorganization with some units fighting to get into the Alps while others were fighting desperately to prevent us from doing the same. They were without sufficient supplies and ammunition and had little or no communications left. One captured German staff officer told us that the only way they knew where their forward units were was to intercept our messages reporting enemy contacts! By that time most of our messages were being sent in the clear because things were moving so fast there was little time to encode and decode them.

During operations through the month of April the original units of the 101st Cavalry Group had suffered 126 casualties and taken the amazing total of over 17,000 prisoners. The large number presented a problem in itself to the Group. It could no longer provide escorts to take them to the rear, but could merely direct them to the nearest corps or division collecting points. It is a conservative estimate that the Germans were losing at least 30 killed and wounded to our one. Why in God's name did the madman in his bunker in Berlin let the slaughter of his own people continue?

Now German defenses had lost all coordination but here and there enough isolated SS units continued the stubborn defense of roadblocks and strong points to make life still uncertain for the men in the lead cavalry detachments. Hour after hour, day after day they had to overcome a special type of fear – fear of the unknown. Where, when and how they would next be met by enemy fire. From machine guns behind the next knoll, hill or river line? Or from panzer faust rockets fired from the next farmhouse or clump of wood? Would a deadly 88 pick off the lead vehicle from a village wall a thousand yards away or would they be caught in a cross fire as they entered the next defile? What was around the next bend in the road and when would they be blown to bits by an AT mine? These men deserve great credit.

Now, as the columns pressed on, the best way the Germans had to delay the advance for more than few hours was to destroy the many bridges along the routes. This required the advance detachments to call up and wait for engineers with bridging equipment to arrive and repair them.

After the fighting around Ammer See the next obstacle to be surmounted was the Loisach River eight miles to the east. In order to cross it the group had to make a long detour to the north, cross into the zone of the 4th Infantry Division and use a bridge repaired by their engineers at Wolfratshausen. Within seven more miles there was another delay while a bridge over the Isar river south of Bad Tolz was repaired by engineers of the 36th Infantry Division.

From 1 May to 4 May the direction and nature of the group's advance changed several times—advancing in front of the 12th Armored Division, protecting its flanks, patrolling and attempting to seize bridges. The 101st Recon Squadron was again attached to the 4th Division where it was engaged in route reconnaissance and screening missions. The remainder of the group continued east and after A Troop of the 116th seized the only intact bridge over the Inn river vicinity of Rosenheim, crossed the river behind it.

On 4 May the group was detached from 12th Armored Division and reverted to XXI Corps control. At the same time the 92nd Recon Squadron reverted back to its parent unit, the 12th Armored. In our 30 days with the division we had worked together as a close-knit team. Most of its senior officers had been cavalrymen and knew its capabilities and how to use it. In turn we were reluctant to see the 92nd under Lieutenant Colonel Sherburne Whipple leave us. They had become as one of our own.

XXI Corps directed the remainder of the group, now with only the 116th and the 342nd AFA Battalions, to proceed east via the Munich-Salzburg autobahn, contact the 2nd French Armored Division and then turn south into the mountain passes of the Alps along the Austrian border.

It appeared that der Fuhrer would not surrender until every inch of German soil was occupied. That was what we were obligingly trying to do for him as fast as possible. It also seemed that his dream of a National Redoubt was just that—a dream

The advance down the autobahn will long be remembered. It would seem that the entire Seventh Army was going east hell-bent-for-election down both east and westbound lanes, while a continuous stream of German prisoners trudged west down the medial strip. Now they were no longer surrendering as individuals but by entire units.

After three months of constant movement our columns had taken on a less military but much more interesting appearance. DPs of all nationalities often hitched rides atop the vehicles. Now and then a black top hat or a spiked old type German helmet appeared from a tank or armored car turret, adding a touch of GI humor. Various types of captured German vehicles were scattered along the column. For a while one troop had adopted a life-sized female mannikin wearing nothing but a fancy ladies' hat as she rode jauntily along in a jeep. Another outfit had liberated a warehouse full of white sheepskin coats intended for Luftwaffe pilots. These they wore with pride and comfort. Now and then a box looking suspiciously like a case of champagne or cognac was seen tied to the back of a vehicle. All the men and vehicles were the color of mud or dust depending on the weather.

Nevertheless, the cavalry columns appeared as thought they had just come off the drill field compared to the sight we saw soon after reaching the autobahn when the entire 2nd French Armored Division came barreling along. It had been equipped by the U.S. Army with enough equipment for a normal armored division but they had commandeered, wangled and liberated enough French, British, German and U.S. vehicles to provide for a division twice that size. They traveled in a variety of uniforms and with great elan accompanied by the women of their choice who waved happily from the trucks they rode in. However, the payoff was that they were a real fighting outfit, eager to make "la Boche" pay for the four year occupation of France.

SECTION 13

THE LAST DAYS OF THE WAR

IN a message dated 0700 4 May, while still on the autobahn, the group received a XXI Corps message through 12th Armored Division which read as follows:

> General Kesselring is expected to surrender forces tonight or tomorrow. In the event he or his emissaries contact our units, they will be conducted by fastest available means to CP 503 Inf. In Munich at eight one seven five eight zero (map coordinates). Notify this Hq.

The long expected news had arrived (we thought)!

Soon after reaching Obersiegsdorf the group left the autobahn and turned south along the Traun River corridor leading directly into the Alps. "A" Troop of the 116th led the advance, but still against stubborn SS resistance. By nightfall 4 May the troop had gotten as far as Seehaus but there it was stopped cold by a blown bridge and SS troops heavily defending roadblocks. We had been unfortunate in having to face the mainstay of SS forces in the Seventh Army Front— the 13th SS Corps, commanded by SS General Max Simon, all the way from the Rhine River.

The morning of 5 May the Group was attached to 101st Airborne Division, General Maxwell Taylor commanding, and at the same time the 101st Recon Squadron reverted back to the Group. At that time the 116th had reached Seegatierl and Marquartstein in the Traun River valley and elements of the 101st Recon Squadron were located in Kossen and Koppel in the Grosse Ache River corridor. The Group CP was located at Rupholding in the next valley west of Hitler's famous "Eagle's Next" at Berchesgaden. There the following message was received:

> "German Army this sector has surrendered. All units remain in place."

This clinched it, the war was really over!

Hitler had never surrendered, but had left this humiliating job up to his generals. Early the morning of 30 April in Berlin he had placed a pistol in his mouth and blown his brains out.

Since the German command was out of communications with many of its forward units some of them continued to fight on. Realizing this, CG 101st Airborne Division issued instructions that all U.S. units would send out parties to inform German commanders of the surrender, advise them of the terms and designate assembly areas for their troops. Our units were then to garrison all large towns and establish military government. Accordingly, the two squadrons and the 342nd AFA Battalion were assigned areas of responsibility for a total of approximately 300 square miles.

In the meanwhile, in the vicinity of Marquartstein, an emissary from the 13th SS Corps was met by the 101st Recon Squadron with a message stating that the SS under Obergrupenfuhrer SS General Gottlieb Berger was not bound by the surrender of General Kesselring's Army Group "G"! He was therefore contacted and escorted to General Taylor at the CP of 101st Airborne Division. There he finally accepted the same terms as Army Group "G." These terms were "unconditional." Now the damn war was over for sure in the entire Seventh Army Sector!

The work of disarming the Germans and attempting to establish military government in the areas just conquered was begun. As can be imagined the entire country was in complete chaos, particularly in the larger towns where Allied bombing and shelling had destroyed transportation and all other public utilities. Most of the Nazi officials and technicians who had governed and operated these towns had either fled or gone underground for fear of arrest. There were shortages of food and other necessities. Looting was rampant, not only by Germans but by Allied troops also.

The days following the surrender became a time of celebrity hunting. Many of the German officials had sought refuge in the Bavarian Alps which could give some credence to the idea of the National Redoubt. Allied units seemed to be competing to see which ones could round up the most of these people.

Based on information that Marshals Goering and Kesselring might be somewhere south of the 101st Cavalry zone of operations it was directed that a unit be dispatched to locate them. Major Edward French, Ex O of the 116th with one platoon of A Troop, Staff Sergeant

Schnalzer in command, was given the mission. Extracts of Major French's after action report telling of the remarkable adventures on this mission are included in Annex 1. It indicates the excellent judgment and diplomacy this young and relatively junior officer exercised in dealing with Swiss, German and Japanese officials, a Hungarian Baroness, a count and senior U.S. Army officers.

On 9 May the 101st Cavalry Group was directed to move farther south into the Alps to control the movement of thousands of prisoners to the various holding areas established by XXI Corps. It also supervised stockpiling of German vehicles, weapons, ammunition and supplies. At Kossen, group headquarters had the unique experience of living in the same small town as the headquarters of the 13th SS Corps. It was not a love feast by any means but many of us had an opportunity to converse and compare notes with some of the SS staff officers. It was here that the 342nd AFA Battalion and an overworked platoon of the 119th Engineers were detached from the group. These units had become smooth working elements of the combined arms team of mechanized cavalry, artillery and engineers and, as with the 92nd Recon Squadron, we were sorry to see them go.

As the war wound down it is well to say something of the men who did so much and we heard of so little. Writers, historians, photographers and newsmen record and glorify the front line fighting men and their commanders, but are prone to neglect those who make it possible for them to fight successfully. These are the people of the medical, supply, communications, maintenance and ordnance elements who kept the fight machine oiled and running. With the lines of supply extended from the French and Belgian ports to the battle lines deep in Germany it was a back-breaking, 24-hour-a-day job to keep the ammunition supplied, the men fed, the wounded evacuated and the weapons and vehicles in good repair. Our squadron supply and maintenance elements were extremely vulnerable to ambush as they shuttled back and forth from supply points, ammunition depots and POL points to the forward units. It is right and proper that these men as well as those who fired the weapons be given full credit for what they did.

SECTION 14

OCCUPATION DUTY

ON 12 May the 101st Cavalry left the scene of its final combat operations and was relieved of assignment to 101st Airborne Division with orders to take up occupation duty in the Odenwald Forest–a familiar area. The group CP was initially set up at Erbachin, the center of the beautiful forest but soon moved farther west to Juggenheim at the edge of the Rhine River valley. Here the troops settled in for an uneasy stay–no one knew for how long. The thought that hung like a cloud over most of us was the prospect of deployment to the Pacific Theater. Some organizations were already being sent there.

Our one military government-trained officer, Major E. L. Harris, had worked like a Trojan as we passed through dozens of towns, but obviously could not handle the large area of the Odenwald. Fortunately, a small military government detachment soon arrived to set up shop. This detachment provided experts in government and public utilities, but the job of carrying out the many tasks rested with our troopers. Occupation regulations were posted and enforced. Travel was restricted and shortages of food and vital equipment had to be rectified. More important was the search for Germans who were capable of re-establishing a working government. General Eisenhower had decreed that no Nazis would be permitted back into government jobs and this made the task more difficult. It will be recalled that General George Patton was relieved of command of the Third U.S. Army because he considered the restoration of control of their own government a first priority and continued to recruit the most capable Germans–Nazi or not–to do the job. (The other reason Patton was relieved is because he continued to sound off about the Russians and was all for continuing on to Moscow.)

The strict policy of non-fraternization established by the U.S. Army with the Germans, particularly with the plentiful, friendly young frauleins, was understood, but was certainly unpopular. As time went on this policy became to come apart at the seams with the help of cigarettes, candy and other gifts.

Almost immediately after the surrender, discipline in the U.S. Army began to deteriorate badly and a groundswell of resentment began to grow because the men were not being sent home quickly enough. In June and July almost daily demonstrations occurred in Frankfurt, 50 miles to our north. The G.I.s didn't seem to realize that there were not enough ships and planes to get them all home at once since shipping priority was being given to the defeat of Japan. To the great credit of the 101st Cavalrymen they continued to retain their morale and discipline.

Soon the worst fears of the men became a reality. Both squadrons were alerted at different times for movement to the Pacific Theater of Operations. My sources are not clear as to the exact dates they left Germany, but it was during late July or in August. They were directed to first go to Camp Campbell, Kentucky to prepare for redeployment to the Pacific, but either while there or en-route, orders were cancelled. They were both saved by the bell when Hiroshima as bombed followed by the Japanese surrender on 15 August 1945. The squadrons were deactivated at Camp Campbell instead and each man was sent to the station nearest to his home for discharge. Others of us had been sent home from Germany individually in early August. Group Headquarters and Headquarters Troop did not leave Germany until later. On 10 October it moved to Camp Heebert, Tarrington, France thence to Le Havre for embarkation to Boston and from there to Camp Miles Standish, Massachusetts. There the unit was deactivated on 30 October 1945. Colonel McClelland had been reassigned to Headquarters Seventh Army in Heidelberg and was the last member of the group to leave Germany. He recalls standing on a sidewalk in Juggenheim waving as the last units pulled out. "Mac" had been an aggressive, hard-driving officer who kept continuous pressure on the Germans throughout the campaign. On the fast-moving, ever-changing battlefront his decisions were quickly made and seldom if ever wrong. The 101st Cavalry could not have had a better wartime leader.

Thus ends the story of the 101st Cavalry's preparation for tour of Europe, courtesy of Uncle Sam.

ANNEX A

THE REMARKABLE ADVENTURES OF MAJOR FRENCH

On 8 May Major Edward French with one platoon of the 116th Recon Squadron was directed to search for Marshal's Goering and Kesselring thought to be in the area to the south. Following are extracts of his after action report.

When we received our mission, I was unable to locate anyone with knowledge of the best route. Therefore, we took off in the direction of Berchesgaden and then headed due south.

The platoon reached Zell Am See at approximately 1500 to find everything quiet. We learned that at the main hotel a German military staff was billeted.

Captain Hellman (interpreter) and I went to the hotel and after questioning we learned from a German officer that a train which contained Field Marshal Kesselring and his staff plus accompanying troops was at Saalfelden RR Station. The patrol immediately went to Saalfelden, located the train, and Captain Hellman and I reported to the Adjutant and explained that we were to see that the Field Marshal and his staff were held in protective custody. The Adjutant brought us to the car of Field Marshal Kesselring and explained our mission to the Field Marshal and General Winters, Chief of Staff, and they agreed that no attempt to leave the train would be made by the Field Marshal or any of his staff. At approximately 0930 a small patrol was dispatched to the castle at Bruck to see what was happening there. Upon arrival an American officer was contacted and it was learned that Goering and family with Goering's staff surrendered to the commanding general, 36th Infantry Division in the castle at 2200 the previous night.

At about 1430 a major from the 101st Airborne Infantry Division arrived and said he had instructions from Commanding General 101st Airborne Division to make arrangements for Kesselring and certain members of his staff to be taken to 101st Airborne Headquarters at Berchesgaden. However, the major didn't make much progress. General Winters, speaking for the Field Marshall, insisted that

Marshall Kesselring was entitled to confer with an American official other than a local commander. At the end of the day no one knew what was to be done with the Field Marshal.

General Taylor, accompanied by his G3 and interpreter, arrived at 0920 the next morning and were shown to the Field Marshal's car. Shortly thereafter the G3 gave me the following instructions, "You and your platoon will move to Bagastein immediately. We have information that the Japanese Embassy, German Secretary of Economics, Secretary of Agriculture and other German officials are located here.

At 1000 the platoon was organized and on the road for Bagastein. We arrived at Badgastein at approximately 1230 and immediately established two blocks on the entrances to the town from the south. Captain Hellman, Sergeant Stutzmand and I immediately went to the Swiss Embassy to secure information as to who was in the town and in the vicinity. The Ambassador and his wife and Mrs. Buchmuller, a member of the staff who spoke English, were very happy to see us and very hospitable. Mrs. Buchmuller arranged for the Japanese Ambassador to come to the hotel and also for the Chief of the German Foreign Office, Von Dornberg, to come to see us. Von Dornberg arrived at 1400. I instructed him to give us a list of all men who had anything to do with the German government, civilian or military and that, furthermore, none of these people, including their staffs, would leave their hotels.

Mr. Uchida, First Secretary of the Japanese Embassy, arrived at 1430 and explained he was very sorry that the Ambassador was not present, but he was not feeling well. Mr. Uchida was informed he would secure a list showing all members of the Embassy, down to the last child, and that no one was to leave their hotels. On the way to the Burgermeister's office we were stopped by an elderly lady and a young man. The lady was Baroness Adele Bornemisza of Hungary. The man was a Hungarian count. The baroness called us aside and told us, secretly, she needed our assistance—that there was a train in the vicinity which contained valuables belonging to the Hungarian government valued at approximately $25,000,000 and that Nazi soldiers had made several attempts to loot the train. Things were getting complicated!

We took the baroness's name and hotel and told her we would see her later! When we met the burgermeister we gave him the usual instructions on curfew, weapons, etc. (weapons had already been collected.) He would issue instructions that no one would leave the town. After more conversation we learned that Mr. Franz Wagenleitner, the burgermeister, and others in the town, were instigating a movement in Austria to free Austria of German rule and set up a free Austrian government. Things were really getting complicated!

When we secured the lists from the Japanese Embassy we found that the Embassy consisted of the Japanese Ambassador Mr. Ashida, family and members of his staff and their families–a grand total of 137. Lists of the German officials revealed the following prominent people:

Secretary of State in the Reichsministry of Agriculture:
  Willekens
Reichsminister and Chief of the Reichschancellery: Harnaike
Chief of the Reichschancellery: Dr. Lammers
Reichsminister of Economics and president of Reichsbank: Dr.
  Funk
Postmaster General: Dr. Ohnesorge
Chief of the German Foreign Office: Van Dornberg.

The following morning at approximately 0800 I was walking through the streets to go to the Swiss Embassy to try and get further information on the story Baroness Bornemisza gave me about the train, when suddenly I was approached by a man of large frame who took my arm and quickly whisked me into a nearby hotel and asked me to be seated. The man, who spoke little English, introduced himself as Nemeth Sandor, the Austrian wrestler. (He had wrestled in the U.S.–I remember seeing a match.) He said he was at present acting as Secretary to Dr. Tobias Kornel, official of the Hungarian government. He said they knew the location of this train and were very much interested in seeing that it was taken over by the American forces, since Nazi officials were trying to confiscate the valuables. Things were getting more and more complicated!

A small patrol was sent to the village of Brockstein to search for the train. When we contacted the station master he said there was a tunnel nearby and that there were six locomotives and nine cars in it and that the locomotives were inoperative.

A Dr. Avar was contacted and he had papers showing exactly what the train contained. The Austrian went with us into the tunnel and we walked for approximately 3 ½ miles before locating the cars. All of the cars were sealed and three locomotives were deadheaded on each end. One car was opened to verify the fact that they did contain something of value. I inspected the contents of this one car and it contained oil paintings, tapestries and rugs. As little as I knew about such values I was satisfied that the remainder of the cars were as reported by Dr. Avar. At approximately 1500 two officers from CIC of XII Corps arrived and began the task of collecting those officials who might be wanted by the Allied Government.

At 2000 the EO of the 101st Cavalry Group, Lieutenant Colonel Mortenson, arrived and explained we were to be relieved that night but that he wanted additional information on the situation. Therefore, it was decided to investigate the train further. At 2030 one platoon from Company "A", 506th Parachute Infantry Battalion, arrived to relieve the platoon of Troop "A." Colonel Mortenson, Major French and Captain Wood went to the train to verify the contents. Four cars were opened and Colonel Mortenson checked two cars which contained silverware, jewelry, etc. and Captain Wood checked two cars which contained rugs, tapestry and oil paintings.

At 0820 the platoon of Troop "A" left Badgastein to rejoin the Squadron at St. Ulrich, thus ending a most interesting experience for all.

ANNEX B

101ST CAVALRY GROUP
OFFICERS ROSTER

O/A 1 March 1945

GROUP HQ AND HQ TROOP
Colonel McClelland, C.B. Co.
Lieutenant Colonel Mortenson, Leo W. * Ex O

Major
    Nawn, Leo J.S2
    Gravdon, Charles K. * SE
    Sweeney, Mercer W. S4

Captain
    Kohnle, Walter R. * Asst S3
    Bissland, Howard R. Ln O
    Eastman, Erick E. Ch
    Powers, Maurice E. Ch
    Cabakoff, Isadore Dentist
    Arnold, Walter R. CO Hq Tr

1st Lt
    Probst, Alan R. Adj
    Paquett, Ray R. Ln O
    Camp, Harry H. Dentist
    Gardner, George T. Ln O

101ST CAVALRY RECONNAISSANCE SQUADRON
Lieutenant Colonel Kendall, Milton * CO

Major
    Brock, Henry J. * Ex O
    Wadsorth, Wm. P. * S3

SQUADRON A

Captain
    Downer, Halsey S. * S2
    Gates, Chester M. S4
    Ritchie, Ralph K. CO A Tr
    Friedman, Abraham CO B Tr
    Bieles, August C. Co C7R
    Thrift, Henry S. Co ETR
    Dykes, Sam Co F CO
    Cubbedge, Edwin W. Motor O
    Kramer, Aaron S. Med O

1st Lieutenant
    Graner, James R.
    McArdle, Charles P.
    Marshall, James W.
    Doubleday, Elwyn J.
    Wright, Arthur E.
    Sullivan, John M. CO B Tr (later)
    Wolkowich, Michael
    Ulmschneider, Robert W. * CO A Tr (later)
    Fabert, Marvin C.
    Pretty, Loren J.
    Perlson, Milton C.
    Jensen, Walter W.
    Geary, Cornelius

2nd Lieutenant
    Goldner, Bernard
    Coady, Tobias F.
    Smith, Kenneth R.
    Mills, Fred L.
    Diemer, Roland M.
    Wilkins, Fred
    Muckstadt, John J.
    Andrew, Wm. C.
    Mathey, Robert F.
    Fabian, Bernard
    Pierce, Charles W.
    Willemain, Bernard M.

CWO Macoratti, Gino A.
WOJG Bunting, Elmer E.
Ogden, Alfred A.

116th CAVALRY RECONNAISSANCE SQUADRON
Lieutenant Colonel Leonard, Hubert C. * CO

Major
    Feagin, Robert D. Ex O
    French, Edward A. * S3

Captain
    Bages, Francis X. * S2
    Weinheimer, William * S4
    Spill, Clarence B. Como O
    Gates, Chester M. Motor O
    Cowen, Louis MC
    Olenick, Irwin H. MC
    Wood, Leslie C. CO Hq Tr
    Burgess, Albert F. CO A Tr
    Littleton, Augustine B. CO B Tr
    Bossert, Louis V. * CO C Tr
    Bell, Edward C. CO E Tr
    Ackerman, Clyde H. CO F Co

1st Lieutenants
    Harden, George W.
    Mann, Ezra B.
    Lewis, Leslie R.
    Langton, George P.
    Reale, Francis V.
    Amos, Stephen F.
    Gaumond, George W.
    Innerarity, Lewis A.
    Greenlaw, Ralph W.
    Perkins, Edwin J.
    Christie, Gustave R.

2nd Lieutenants
    Mayes, Louis T.

Gordon, Benjamin D.
Schafer, Robert K.
Bobo, James C.
Mack, Frederick N.
Wood, Harvey E.
Borkowski, Joseph
Betwy, Andrew L.
Dees, Joe
Hasley, John S.
McCreedy, William J. *
Pierce, Charles N.
CWO Tobie, Louis J.
WOJG Farrell, Edward J.
Brett, Raymond F.

NOTES:
(1) * with 101st when federalized January 1941
(2) Records of assignments of lieutenants not available

APPENDIX III

HORSE ACTIVITIES PROGRAM
1949-1950

Introduced by Lieutenant Colonel Frederick L. Devereux

I. <u>GENERAL RIDING</u>: During the summer just past, all horses considered unsuitable were disposed of. The balance of the string was sent to summer pasture for three months and have returned rejuvenated and ready to provide good riding. Twenty new mounts have been added to the stable, bringing the total up to 55 good horses– an assortment from which we feel any beginner or advanced rider can be suitably mounted.

Ten of the new horses were selected as outstanding mounts for riders of some experience–any ex-horse trooper would feel thoroughly at home with them. They average under eight years, are well-schooled, well-mouthed and are a hunter type. Several are better than average jumpers. The remaining ten are registered Morgans– ideal for anyone up to 150 pounds–particularly children and beginning ladies, for whose use they were especially selected. They have all been ridden, jumped and shown by children, have excellent manners and good gaits.

A. <u>Eligibility to Ride</u>: The following persons are authorized to ride Squadron A Association-owned horses:
1. Ex-members
2. Active members
3. Families and guest
4. Members of riding classes

B. Riding pass: All persons riding in Central Park and <u>all active members at any time outside of riding class</u>, must present a riding pass to the stable manager before mounting. (Occasional guests, when accompanied by a member, will be excepted from this regulation.)

Riding passes will be issued automatically, upon application, to
1. Ex-horse troopers
2. Members of the family of pass holders
3. Guests sponsored by pass holders

Pass holders who request riding privileges be extended to guests and members of their family must certify that the applicants are qualified riders and must further assume responsibility for their conduct while riding.

Ex-members who are not automatically qualified for a riding pass may ride in the ring during hours reserved for general riding and will normally find present, on Friday evenings and Saturday and Sunday afternoons, an officer designated to give instruction to those requesting it. The officer in charge of the ring during these hours will be authorized to give riding passes to applicants demonstrating a satisfactory proficiency.

All active riding passes outstanding have been revoked. A new numbered pass is being is as of 15 September. Examination for active member riding pass will be conducted during the hours enumerated in the preceding paragraph and also after certain drill nights to be announced.

<u>There is no charge for a riding pass. If you are eligible but have lost your old one or if you want a pass issued to family or guests, fill in the application attached to this memorandum.</u>

C. Hours: Ring – Monday   - 3:00-6:00
                     Friday   - 3:00-5:30; 7:30-10:30
                     *Saturday - 9:00-12:00; 1:00-5:30
                     Sunday   - 9:00-12:00; 1:00-5:30

*due to children's classes, one half of the ring is open to general riding on Saturdays between 10:00-12:00

Park –   Daily, weather permitting, 9:00 AM until dark

Active members may ride after drill, subject to regulations posted in Troop orderly rooms.

D. <u>Charges</u>: Active members, after drill $0.50
          " " ,   other riding $1.00
          " " ,   family and guest $1.50
          Ex-members $2.00
          " " ,   family and guest $2.00

E. <u>Reservations</u>: Accepted up to 24 hours in advance. Call Atwater 9-6020; ask for "Stables." Horses may be reserved by name but will not beheld after the reserved time.

F. <u>Method of Payment</u>: The book-ticket system has been reinstated — <u>cash will no longer be accepted at the stable office</u>. Ticket books may be obtained by mail use attached coupon), or during office hours, at the Armory office which closes Saturday noon.

Ticket books are sold in units of $5.00 and a 10 percent discount is given on purchase of two or more books at any one time.

All books are numbered and registered in the name of the owner. They are <u>not</u> transferable. Refunds will be given on all unused tickets at any time up to one year after issue date, upon application.

II <u>RIDING CLASSES</u>

In the past eight years a shortage of horses made necessary the curtailment of riding classes at Squadron A. With the weeding out of unsuitable horses and the addition of 20 good mounts we are once again in the position to offer expert instruction and good horses with a choice of hours to accommodate beginning and advanced children and ladies, beginning active members and advanced active and ex-members who desire jumping instruction.

The schedules and classes listed below are tentative, as are the instructors. These classes will be held if a minimum enrollment is obtained, otherwise consolidation with other classes will be affected.

<u>Priority for all classes will be given to applications received before 1 October. Applications will be numbered in order of their receipt. No class will contain more than 30 members and a waiting list will be established beginning with number 31. Students absent for other</u>

than medical reasons for more than two consecutive lessons may be dropped in favor of persons on the waiting list.

A. Children: For the past several years we have not been able to accommodate many children who wanted to learn to ride due to two principal factors—a shortage of horses and a lack of instructors. Now, with the addition of 10 Morgans (which are ideal for beginning children) plus several other new horses selected with children in mind, as well as the retention of several old favorites from last years' class, we can mount as many as 30 children per class and have each child suitably mounted. Instructors of experience and outstanding reputation have been secured for each class.

1. Eligibility: Children between the ages of 11½ and 17½ on 1 October 1949 are eligible for Squadron A riding classes. Children under 11½ who were members of last year's classes and other exceptions should be brought to attention of Horse Officer. Preferences in oversubscribed classes will be determined in accordance with the following priority:

A. Children of active or ex-members
B. 1948-49 waiting list
C. Relatives of active or ex-members

1. Schedule: Classes will commence the week of 9 October. Preference for the Saturday morning class will be given to children non-residents of Manhattan and those whose school schedules preclude mid-week attendance. Experience leads to the suggestion that your child stands a much better chance of being accepted for a Wednesday or Thursday afternoon class than on Saturday morning. Please avoid registering for the Saturday class if at all possible.

Wednesday	-	Advanced, 3:30;	Basic, 4:30
Thursday	-	Advanced, 3:30;	Basic, 4:30
Saturday	-	Advanced, 10:00;	Basic, 11:00

It is suggested that children under the age of 15 should initially be enrolled in the basic class. Instructors will shift children between classes as they progress or show need for more basic instruction. A total of 24 lessons - followed by a horse show - will be given. Classes will be suspended during the holidays.

2. <u>Instructors</u>: Colonel Samuel V. Constant, Cavalry, USA Retired. Major H. M. Bowlby, Jr., Cavalry, USA and Captain Claude Viollet, French Army, Retired.

Colonel Constant, well-known to many members of the Squadron and a prominent equitation judge at metropolitan area horse shows, is a graduate of Fort Riley and has taught equitation both in the Army and at several ROTC colleges. He is particularly interested in teaching children, with great numbers of whom he has had outstanding success.

Major Bowlby is a graduate of West Point and Fort Riley. Before the mechanization of the 11th Cavalry he served as remount officer and recruit instructor. He has been highly recommended as an able instructor.

Captain Viollet served with the regular French cavalry for 10 years pre-Vichy as a troop commander. He is a graduate of Saumur, is currently an instructor at West Point and for the past three years has spent his summers at Ecole Champlain, Ferrisburg, Vermont in charge of the riding instruction of some 200-odd girls.

3. <u>Charges</u>: $60.00 for 24 lessons, payable if desired in two installments, 1 October and 1 February.

B. <u>Ladies</u>: There has been a considerable demand for a ladies riding class – a popular pre-war activity which the recent shortage of suitable horses had made impractical to revive until now. Our new horses enable us to mount both a beginning and advanced class with a suitable horse for every rider.

Ladies under the age of 18 should apply for a children's class.

1. <u>Schedule</u>: Tuesday afternoons. Advanced 3:30; Basic 4:30
2. <u>Instructor</u>: Major Arthur Surcamp, Corps of Engineers USA.

Major Surkamp, a graduate of West Point where he is currently on duty, was captain of the cadet polo team of 1943. He is an outstanding horseman who will be seen riding for the West Point team in the winter polo season at the Armory and has had extensive experience in teaching riding and jumping.

3. <u>Charges</u>: $60.00 for 24 lessons; payable, if desired in installments 1 October and 1 February.

C. <u>Active Members Basic Equitation Class</u>: If you are in the mechanized squadron, have ridden little or not at all and wonder what it's all about – what is there about a horse that so many ex-members get so nostalgic over – this is for you. An equivalent civilian course would cost well over a hundred dollars – this one is six dollars and fifty cents. Here's a "get rich quick" course incorporating all the best instructional methods used at Riley–with instructors who have been through the mill of teaching hundreds of recruits.

You'll saddle and groom your own horse, you'll have to show up every Friday night ready to go at 1930 for thirteen weeks (if you miss two classes in a row a man on the waiting list will take your place), toward the end of the course you'll be expected to do some outside riding on your own. The first four or five sessions will be mighty uncomfortable so don't sign up unless you really mean to see it through. If you stay with it the odds are that you've had a lot of fun by the time it's over, you be able to go out in the park with confidence and you'll be ready to go on and learn to jump.

1. <u>Eligibility</u>: Active members of the 101st Mechanized Cavalry Reconnaissance Squadron NYNG who are not qualified to hold riding passes. First come, first served.
2. <u>Schedule</u>: Friday nights 7:30-9:00
3. <u>Instructors</u>: Lieutenant Colonel Frederick L. Devereux, Jr., Cavalry (ORC); Captain Edward Bimberg, 101st Cavalry: Captain William Stefurak, Cav. (ORC).

Colonel Devereux, an ex-stable sergeant of old E Troop and Horse Officer of A Troop of the 101st at Devens in 1941, is a graduate of the Cavalry School, Fort Riley. He served at USMA, West Point, as cadet equitation instructor, plebe polo team coach, cadet jumping team coach and member of the West Point Horse Show Team.

Captain Bimberg, C.O. of headquarters Troop was also a Devens horse trooper and has been instructing riders at the Squadron for the past three years. He was an outstanding member of last year's horse show team.

Captain Stefurak was a member of the horse squadron at Devens where he was in charge of the remount detail. After graduation from Fort Riley he was assigned to the 1st Cavalry Division where he taught recruit equitation. He too was a leading rider on last year's jump team.

4. <u>Charges</u>: $6.50 (payable with application) for thirteen lessons. A new class will be formed in January 1950 with priority given to the waiting list from the first class.

5. <u>Uniform</u>: Issue shirt, no tie, no headgear. Private or GI breeches may be worn. Boots are preferred but leggings are acceptable. Arrangements may be made through the PX for leggings, breeches and three-buckle boots.

D. <u>Advanced Equitation Class</u>: This class is designed for the rider who qualifies for a park pass, wants to learn to jump properly and to school a horse to jump. For the first few months equitation on the flat will be stressed and no high jumping will take place until both horse and rider are ready. Attention will be concentrated on teaching both horse and rider balance, control and collection.

Each rider will be assigned two horses—one a show team prospect, the other either a green jumper or one needing to be reclaimed. Members of the class will be expected to exercise these horses for a minimum of one hour weekly outside of class.

It is hoped that, from among the active member students, six or eight will develop to the point where a Squadron A. Horse Show Team can be formed for competition in the spring of 1950. Any member of the active organization who desires to compete for a place on the team, if formed, must enroll in the jumping class and attend a satisfactory number of classes.

Aside from the hope of developing riders for a team, the class is intended to give any rider who has the patience not to want to rush beyond his capabilities, a solid jumping seat and knowledge of how to school horses over fences which should make him a better horseman.

Because of the specialized nature of the class with the need for almost individual instruction, the class will be limited to 20.

1. <u>Eligibility</u>: Members of the active organization and Ex-members who hold riding passes.

2. <u>Schedule</u>: Wednesday evenings, 6:00-7:30

3. <u>Instructor</u>: Lieutenant Colonel F. L. Devereux, Jr. Cav (ORC)

4. <u>Charges</u>: $1.00 per session, payable to Team Secretary at each class formation. Students, when selected as Team members, will become exempt from charges.

5. <u>Uniform</u>: Shirts, boots, breeches, spurs.

E. <u>Miscellaneous</u>:

1. <u>Dress Regulations</u>: Gentlemen will wear boots, breeches and coats at all times. Ladies will wear jodhpurs and will wear coats of conservative color and cut. Children will be appropriately dressed. Either a turtleneck sweater or a shirt will be worn. Neckties will be worn with shirts and the Squadron A necktie will <u>not</u> be worn. Spurs optional. Whips will not be carried. <u>Hats will be worn </u>in Central Park between 15 September and 1 May inclusive.

2. <u>Private Mounts</u>: 20 stalls are reserved for horses the property of active or ex-members. Rates: standing stall $60, box $65 per month, subject to revision depending on the price of forage.

APPENDIX IV

ANSWERING THE 9-11 CALL
A New York National Guard Unit
Rushes Into Manhattan's Chaos
by
Major Eric Durr

(From *ARMOR*–January-February 2002)

NEW YORK CITY – the 1st Battalion, 69th Infantry, and the 1st Battalion, 258th Field Artillery – approached the police and put together an *ad hoc* plan to secure southern Manhattan. The three commanders agreed the 1069th Inf and I-101st Cav would establish a security perimeter south of Canal Street, and be relieved by I-258th FA that night.

While their New York City brothers in arms were responding to urgent calls for help, the Soldiers of B, C, and D Companies rallied at their armories and began loading trucks for the move south. Communications with Staten Island were virtually nil, so the XO assumed control of the upstate units and directed C Company, the most remote unit, to move its soldiers and equipment to Troy as quickly as possible. The goal was to muster B and C Companies together and road march south to Staten Island.

Contact was finally made with LTC Costagliola, who directed D Company to move to Staten Island on the New York State Thruway no later than 2000 and instructed the XO and CSM to move B and C as quickly as possible.

With only about 200 soldiers at the Staten Island Armory, the I-101 Cav needed its upstate manpower to complete the mission.

But the B Company and C Company move was delayed. State headquarters refused to issue road clearance for a convoy, or to provide a bus for soldiers who couldn't be carried in military vehicles. The response to the XO's entreaties to move the two companies was that there was no mission request yet.

Complicating the movement request was the fact that the New York National Guard's standing disaster relief C2 arrangements put A, D, and HHC, I-101st Cav subordinate to NYARNG's 53rd Troop Command, while B Company and C Company fell under the geographic region controlled by HQ, 42nd Infantry Division. Direct intervention by the 53rd Troop Command commander finally eliminated the logjam at state headquarters, but by then it was too late to move B Company and C Company that night.

On the morning of September 12, the soldiers of A and D Companies and HHC deployed to Manhattan with the armored HMMWVs of the combined scout/mortar platoon, dubbed Saber Element, leading the way. As he came within sight of the devastated buildings. LTC Costagliola could think only of nuclear war. Lower Manhattan looked like and atomic bomb had gone off, he recalled. The streets were littered with abandoned cars, many with roofs crushed by chunks of concrete. Scraps of gray dust covered everything. Above it all hovered the heavy pall of smoke from the World Trade Center.

Uncertain about what missions they faced, the battalion brought empty trucks, a HEMTT loaded with emergency supplies, wreckers, fuelers, and weapons and riot control equipment stored on locked, built-up five-tons. The fresh soldiers linked up with a 30-member element that ILT Tracey Young, commander of A Company, had brought to Manhattan on the night of September 11 to relieve CPT Willis' contingent.

The I-69th Infantry and I-101st Cav established a line of troops that effectively closed Manhattan Island south of Canal Street and placed assembly areas in Battery Park, at Manhattan's southern tip. Battery Park is usually where tourists line up to buy tickets for trips to the Statue of Liberty. The Park included historic Castle Clinton, built as a harbor fortification in 1808. During the Civil War, New York troops mustered there. Once again it was a military assembly area.

While A, D, and HHC took their positions, B and C Companies were road marching south to link up with the rest of the battalion in Manhattan. The upstate New York soldiers were routed around traffic by the New Jersey State Police and their 20-vehicles convoy was rolling along a deserted highway leading to the Holland Tunnel and Manhattan by 1000. As they approached, they caught glimpses of the gaping hole in the New York City skyline, replaced by a huge, rising cloud of smoke, which was evident for miles away.

The battalion's main mission was to help the New York City Police Department keep gawkers and other non-essential personnel out of Lower Manhattan. With more manpower, I-69th Infantry took the larger perimeter stretching along the west side of Manhattan up to Chambers Street. Broadway was the operational boundary between the two battalions.

Each company was assigned a piece of the screen line. Three to five soldiers, backed up by NYPD members, checked identifications and determined who could enter the so-called "frozen zone."

Among them were the residents who lived in that area. Companies provided soldiers to escort southern Manhattan's apartment dwellers, hurriedly evacuated on September 11, into and out of their homes as they searched for pets, prescriptions, and valuables. The soldiers often provided a comforting shoulder when residents broke down, confronted by the devastation around them.

I-101 Cav also assumed initial responsibility for securing and providing staffing for one of the emergency morgues set up in 1 Liberty Plaza, a massive office building which many rescue workers feared would fall. The battalion's support platoon and maintenance platoon provided details to keep nonessential personnel and the curious from interfering with the battalion medics working inside.

Work on the site was punctuated by periodic warnings that buildings were about to collapse. Everybody quickly learned that three blasts on an air horn meant "Run like hell... something's coming down." There were several false alarms, and by Day Three of the operation, it was SOP that rally points be established for soldiers working near the WTC site and that by-name lists of soldiers on details had to be provided to the TOC for accountability purposes.

Battalion soldiers also conducted a variety of logistics missions. Battalion trucks carried bottled water and jack-hammers from a ferry landing on the Hudson River to the WTC site and provided a water buffalo for FBI agents screening WTC refuse at the Staten Island landfill. The fire department on Staten Island was provided with an M-1064 mortar track to use in blocking an entrance into a critical area, and HEMTT fuelers were stationed on Manhattan to fuel fire department vehicles. Battalion HMMWV's were also used to collect and distribute food prepared by restaurants to feed rescue workers.

Many of the cav unit's soldiers were frustrated because they wanted to go to the WTC site and help dig out survivors. It galled them to read accounts of volunteers from Main or Ohio who were allowed to work at the site. Many of the I-101 Cav soldiers felt a special urgency to help in the rescue effort because the New York City-based members had friends buried in the rubble. Almost a quarter of the battalion's soldiers are police officers and firefighters. They felt the loss of colleagues killed when the buildings collapsed.

But the situation at Ground Zero demanded special expertise in recovery that the battalion's soldiers didn't have. The fire department insisted that the Guardsmen could do more good in a security mission. That was borne out on the night of September 13 when the battalion was asked to come in and perform a crowd control mission at the site.

A massive crane was being erected and the hosts of firemen and police officers on hand to watch and help were getting in the way. At the request of the fire department, the Battalions A and D Companies came in to clear the way and then establish an inner perimeter to keep nonessential, but well-meaning, personnel away. As a "third party," the Guard had authority that neither the cops nor firefighters would have had with each other. The Guard presence also put an end to a lot of well-meaning, but unnecessary, rescue workers freelancing at the site.

With so many unit members in the NYPD or the FDNY, about 100 opted to serve with those city organizations when the I-101st mobilized. Fortunately, many key leaders and soldiers in critical positions, like HHC commander CPT James Horn, and A Company commander 1LT Tracey Young, members of the NYPD, opted to mobilize with the unit.

He mobilized with the I-101st, 1LT Dennis O'Brien (also a lieutenant in the NYPD) explained, because he felt he could do more good as a Guardsman than as a police officer.

O'Brien said that as a police lieutenant, he would show up at a station house and be handed a list of paper with the names of three sergeants and 12 officers he'd never worked with before and told to head out to Manhattan. By serving with the I-101st Cav, he was working with people he knew and who knew him, and with a defined chain of command, he said.

The battalion operation quickly assumed the familiar framework of tactical echelons.

The Manor Road Armory on Staten Island served as the field trains and life support center. A maintenance slice worked here to keep vehicles running and handle logistics reports and paperwork, while the battalion's mess section served meals before shifts and ran lunchtime LOGPAC to troops working in Manhattan. The battalion S4 immediately opened a contract with a local caterer and arranged for laundry services. The S4 section also coordinated the distribution of bottled water, extra food, and clothing and toiletry items donated to the rescue effort by local businesses.

A small slice of HHC soldiers, supplemented by members of the New York Guard, a voluntary state militia organization, provided armory security and ran some logistics support missions from the armory.

The soldiers from B, C, and D Companies were housed in the armory mess hall and classroom while HHC and A Company soldiers crammed themselves into offices. Soldiers who lived on State Island were allowed to go home to make space in the building.

Transportation was arranged through the Metropolitan Transit Authority, which provided buses to move the soldiers to and from Manhattan. An emergency vehicle lane on the Brooklyn Expressway and Staten Island Expressway provide access to Manhattan through the Battery Tunnel.

The battalion also made extensive use of the Staten Island Ferry, which was closed to non-emergency traffic during the first week of the deployment. Each morning the convoy would roll down to the ferry landing and roll onto a waiting boat, which would transport the vehicles and soldiers across New York harbor. LTC Costagliola, referenced the Battle of Stalingrad, began to joke about heading "back across the Volga."

The battalion TOC, housed in a five-ton command van the battalion acquired in lieu of a five-ton truck, was initially co-located with the NYPD emergency operations center at a Pathmark supermarket. The TOC was shared with the I-258th and the initial higher headquarters for Operation NYC, the 107th Support Group, placed a liaison officer there. The TOC was able to coordinate directly with the NYPD, 258th, and 107th to coordinate battalion missions.

Finally, the battalion's TAC was based in the Battery Park area. At this location, the battalion commander could monitor events and reach critical points rapidly. For three days following a rainstorm on September 13, the TAC was established in the Staten Island Ferry terminal, which was closed to non-emergency foot traffic, and the battalion's vehicles parked outside.

A critical concern for the battalion's leadership was obtaining masks so soldiers could filter out the dust and potential carcinogens that filled the air near the WTC site.

Initially, all the battalion had available were dust masks from a Home Depot and filter masks obtained by the C Company Commander, CPT Michael Pickering, from his workplace. As time went on, more efficient masks were made available to all rescue workers and the battalion's soldiers acquired them. Battalion uniform SOP required a protective mask on a soldier's Load Bearing Equipment (LBE). Soldiers working near the WTC site were required to wear their masks.

Even so, a number of unit members reported respiratory problems at the conclusion of the two-week tour. As this article is written, an effort is underway to ensure that Line of Duty (LOD) investigations are conducted for each individual.

Communication was another critical issue for the battalion.

The initial attacked wiped out land line phones and disrupted cell phone systems. On the evening of September 11, the battalion employed the Internet and personal AOL accounts to communicate between Staten Island and Troy, New York. The Internet was first developed as a way to route messages indirectly in a nuclear attack and it worked for the I-101st Cav. E-mailed Sitreps sent by LTC Costagliola from Staten Island to Troy were passed onto the state and 42nd ID Emergency Operation Centers, providing them with timely information on the disaster.

By September 12, cell phone communications began to come back up, although they were not completely reliable. The battalion's leadership relied on personnel cell phones to keep in touch with the rear operation on Staten Island and with each other when FM communications didn't work because of the New York City skyscrapers. The general consensus was that everybody's cell phone bill was going to be immense. A letter was prepared from the battalion commander to send to cell phone providers asking that the charges be waived because of the nature of the emergency.

FM communications were normally reliable. But as an armor unit, the battalion didn't have all the PRC-77 backpack sets that could have been used. The battalion's HMMWVs were pressed into use as command and control vehicles to link together removed security points. With no set SOI the battalion's communications section simply picked frequencies that would not conflict with police and fire radio nets. The battalion employed fixed call signs and operated on 30.00 for the duration of the deployment.

The battalion also pressed its collection of PRC-127 Motorola "brick" radios into service. Obtained mainly to facilitate range operations during tank gunnery, the small radios proved invaluable in linking key personnel together.

The communications system improved immeasurably when State Headquarters provided Nextel cell phones to key leaders in all the committed battalions and headquarters. The system could be employed as a standard cell phone or as a two-way radio and went a long way towards linking together all National Guard elements on the ground in Manhattan.

There was initially some confusion over the battalion's weapons status.

With communication with state headquarters cut off, the battalion commander reacted to the news that the U.S. military was at a high threatcon level by deciding to send the soldiers in under arms.

When the battalion initially deployed, some of the scout HMMWVs had M-2HB and M-60 machine guns mounted and some battalion soldiers were armed. Directives from state headquarters and the governor's office soon made it clear that this was unacceptable. Nevertheless the images of army HMMWVs were broadcast on CNN for several days.

Since the battalion was an Aid to Civil Authorities status, the determination by the New York Adjutant General was that no weapons would be carried. JAG lawyers made it clear that even the battalion's police officer members, who are required to carry weapons when off duty, could not carry their police or personal weapons while in a uniformed status. With reports of possible follow-up terrorist attacks coming regularly during the first week of deployment, the no-weapons rule caused some consternation for battalion soldiers. Lower-ranking police officers also repeatedly expressed surprise that the National Guard soldiers were not armed. "Aren't you guys here to protect us?" one officer asked a battalion soldier at a check point.

Liaison with the police department was critical. MAJ Robert Maganini, an intelligence officer from New Jersey normally working in the 42nd Infantry Division's G-2 section, played a critical role in moving between the police and the deployed battalions during the first few days. He kept police officials informed of Guard capabilities and helped explain police intent to the deployed battalions. Initially, he and a few other officers worked alone, but as the deployment progressed, this *ad hoc* arrangement was formalized, with National Guard liaison officers working in every police zone.

During the first week of operations, the battalion was uncertain about potential missions and deployed each day with a variety of vehicles and equipment. Equipment on hand included weapons, riot control gear and flak vests, along with a variety of picks and shovels. By the second week of Operation NYC, the mission had become one of presence and helping to secure the WTC site, and the battalion began leaving fueling and hauling assets and unneeded HMMWVs at Manor Road.

The battalion benefited from the relationship of many of its soldiers to NYC government. One member of the support platoon was a bus scheduler with the Metropolitan Transit Authority and was invaluable in obtaining and coordinating bus support for the battalion. Other soldiers had connections with the NYPD and FDNY, which came in handy in obtaining supplies.

In the absence of direction from higher headquarters, the three battalion commanders in lower Manhattan pretty much did their own thing, coordinating with each other to ensure all missions were covered. The *ad hoc* arrangement was approved by the 53rd Troop Command commander.

Stress was an issue for the battalion during the deployment. Many of the New York City-area soldiers were dealing with the knowledge that friends and acquaintances were dead in the wreckage of the World Trade Center. Some had narrowly escaped death in the catastrophe themselves. Many of the other soldiers had concerns about being yanked away from home, family, and work at short notice. State headquarters made available a crisis counseling team comprised of a psychiatrist, psychologist and Army social worker, who made themselves readily available to the battalion's soldiers.

The crisis team debriefed all the soldiers prior to rotation home to help deal with the trauma of the things they saw and did for two weeks. In one instance, a soldier was hospitalized overnight for a psychiatric disorder, which the crisis team identified.

As in most National Guard deployments, the issue of civilian job and school conflicts began to become a serious mission distraction for many soldiers. New York National Guard JAG officers were made available by the end of the first week to deal with any employer threat to dismiss a soldier of state Active Duty. As the mission became more routine during the second week, college students were released to return to school.

A key issue for many I-101st Cav members who were police officers was the status of their military leave time. Most government agencies provide 30 days of military leave for civil servants.

Since the battalion had already performed AT in July and August many police officers began using up their leave time and some had to leave the battalion and return to their jobs or face loss of pay or health insurance.

Concern about jobs and rights to jobs resulted in a limited response when the state later asked for volunteers to continue the mission once the battalion deployment ended. Many job protections under state and federal law vanish if a soldier volunteers to go on state Active Duty.

On top of its other missions, the I-101st Cav also carried out information operations in support of the New York National Guard PAO. A team of *New York Times* reporters and photographers lived with the battalion for a week, writing stories about the Guard mission in NYC. LTC Costagliola was featured on an Italian television newscast, and the battalion played host to reporting teams from the *Albany times Union* and *Staten Island Advance*.

For two weeks, the I-101st Cav soldiers performed every mission given them. There were no complaints despite long hours, stressful circumstances, and cramped living conditions.

To a man, the battalion's soldiers were glad they could be doing something to help their fellow citizens and live up to the battalion's motto, "To the Utmost."

Maj. Eric Durr was commissioned in Armor from Kent State University in 1980 and has served as a platoon leader in 2-64 Armor in Germany and assistant S3 of the 479th Engineer Battalion, Watertown, N.Y. He has also served as S2, tank company commander, and headquarters company commander in 1-210 Armor, based in Albany, N.Y. A graduate of the reserve Armor Officer Advanced Course and CGSC, he is the executive officer of 1-101 Cav, based in Staten Island, N.Y.

SQUADRON A MEMBERS

ACCORDINO, William A.
ACHENBACH, Benjamin R.
ADAMS, Mr. John L.
ADLER, James A.
AGREN, Barbara J.
AGUIAR, Ms Christiana
AKES, John K.
ALBANO, Mrs. Salvatore
ALDRICH Jr., Richard S.
ALDRICH, Mr. Frank N.
AMATRUDO, Maj. Emanuel J.
AMBROSE Jr., Stephen F.
ANDERSON, Maj. Gen. Andrew H.
ANDERSON, Michael J.
ANDERSON, Mrs. Leroy
ANIKEEFF, Anthony H.
ANIKEEFF, Michael A.
ANIKEEFF, Nicholas M.
AREND, Geoffrey
ARMITAGE, Arthur L.
ASVAZADOURIAN, Edward
ATTERBURY, Mr. Boudinot P.
AULT, Bromwell
AUSTIN Jr., William E.
AUSTIN, Anita P.
BABCOCK, Jeffrey
BACKUS, Richard
BAER JR., Theodore C.
BAKER, Elizabeth M.
BAKER, Hayden S.
BAKER, James B.
BAKER, James M.
BAKER, John Milnes
BALCO, George J.
BALLARD, Elizabeth F. R.
BALLARD, Robert F. R.
BALLARD, Wendy F. R.
BANFIELD, Duncan S.
BANKS Jr., C. Whitney

BAREFOOT, Paul D.
BARKER, Mr. George E.
BARNETT, Mr. Augustus C
BARRETT, Matilda J. W.
BARRY, Capt. Raymond A.
BEARCE, Maj. Maynard
BEARCE, Mrs. Herbert
BEDDER Jr., Arthur J.
BEGLAN Jr., John L.
BELL, Christopher D.
BELLER, Gary A.
BENDER, Peter
BENEDICT, Bruce W.
BENICHOU, Jennifer A.
BENJAMIN, Samuel N.
BENJAMIN, Stephen N.
BENSLEY, Bruce N.
BENSON, James D.
BENSON, Judith Gilkes
BENT, Col. Peter W.
BERCOVITZ, Col. G. E.
BERGER, Martin L.
BETZ III, Otto J.
BIAYS Jr., John S.
BIGELOW, Ernest A.
BILLETT, Michael E.
BIMBERG, Edward L.
BIRD, Deborah
BISSET, Alfred G.
BISSET, Capt. Andrew E.
BOLLES, William W.
BOLTER, Eugene
BONDY, Col. Lance H.
BOOTH, Cinnamon Anne
BORN, Emelie S.
BOWDEN, Garret R.
BOYAR, Burton A.
BRADY, Anne Dallett
BRADY, Gertrude A.

BRADY, Philip H.
BRANDOLINO, Bonnie
BRAWER, Nicholas A.
BRENNAN, Capt. Lawrence
BRENNAN, Patrick A.
BRENNAN, Patrick J.
BRICKLEY Jr., Richard L.
BRINCKERHOFF, Natalie G.
BRITTON, Thomas B.
BRODBECK, Mary C.
BROOKER Jr., Robert E.
BROWN, Col. Edward D.
BROWN, Col. Stewart J.
BRUCE, Capt Michael Ian
BRYCE, David A.
BUCHET, Michael M. X.
BUCK, Mrs. Thomas M.
BUICE III, William T.
BURLING, Andrew G.
BURNS, John E,
BURNS, Michael
BUTLER, John R.
BUTLER, Jonathan P.
BYRNE Sr., Donn H.
CABELL, Ellen
CAFFREY, Elise P
CAMPAIGN, H. John
CAMPBELL, MG Donald F.
CAMPBELL, Mr. John C. E.
CAMPBELL, Samuel R
CANNON, Alexander
CAREY, Francis J.
CARMICHAEL, Joseph R.
CARR, LCDR Michael F.
CARRIG Jr., Maj. John T.
CARTMELL, CWO Henry T.
CASHMAN, Peter
CASS, L Winship Cook
CHABRIER, Yvonne
CHAMBERS, Austin
CHATEAUVERT, Julie
CHERASHORE, Matthew J.
CHESTER, J. Chapman
CHIPMAN, Gordon L

CHITTIM, Gordon M.
CHOP, Christopher E.
CHRISTMAN, LTG Daniel W.
CIAFFA, Philip R.
CLAIBORNE, David W.
CLARE III, William F.
CLARE IV, William
CLARE, John E.
CLARK Jr., Mrs Charles M.
CLARK, Anthony
CLAWSON, Harry Q. M.
COLLINS III, Henry L.
COLLINS Jr., MG William J.
COLT, MG Richard S.
COMSTOCK, Lawrence A.
CONANT, Cynthia W.
CONLON, Robert K.
CONNELLY III, John E
CONNELLY, Christopher
CONNOR, Keith F.
CONSTABLE, Henry L.
CONSTABLE, Ms Elise J.
COOK, Anthony P.
COOPER, Mr. John L.
CORT, John
COSGROVE, John P.
COSTAGLIOLA, LTC Mario
COSTELLO, Timothy M.
COTTER, Col. Chester F.
COUGHLIN, P. Kent
COX, S. Roger
COX, Sean C.
COYNE, LTC James M.
CRAGOE, Dr. Carol Davidson
CRITES, Sherman E
CROSSMAN, Edgar O.
CROSSMAN, Patrick F.
CRUTCHER, William C.
CUNNINGHAM, LTC Daniel R.
CUPSCHALK, CDR John F. V.
CURRIER, Elizabeth B
CUSHMAN Jr., Paul
CUTSHAW, Kenneth A
D'ANTIN, Duke Alba-Teran

DALE, Madeline
DALE, Nancy W.
DALLEN Jr., Russell M.
DALVA II, Col. David L.
DAVID, William S.
DAVIDSON, Patricia F.
DAVIES, Robert N.
DAY, Nathaniel B.
DE SALVO, Lt. Andrew J.
DE VIENNE, Count Arnaud
DEAN, Charles C.
DEVEREAUX, Foster,
DIEFENBACH M.D., W. Paul
DISPENZIERI, Eileen, S
DONALD, Douglas D,
DONNELLY, Sean J.
DORE Jr., William F.
DORR, Stephen H
DOTSEY, LTC George J.
DOUGLAS, John
DRECHSLER, Noel Jones
DREW, Sean S.
DRYER Jr., Gregory C.
DUER, Beverly Chew
DUFFY, Vincent R.
DUNHAM Jr., William P.
DUNHAM, Edith
DUNNING Jr., A. R.
DURANT, Richard
DURR, L. Col. Eric
DURYEA, Mr. John C.
EASMAN Jr., William S.
ELIOT, Lawrence H.
ELKUS, Gretchen M.
ELLENBERG, Jane Victor
ELLIOT Jr., Henry P.
ELTING, John W.
ELTING, Margaret C.
EMMET, Herman Leroy
ENGLER Jr., Henry A.
ERTZ, John K.
ESPACH, Robert
ESTERLINE III, John W.
EVANS, Larry A.

EWIG, Thomas A.
EWING, Suzanne
FAHNESTOCK, Marion B.
FAIRCHILD, Freeman
FAIRLEIGH, Kenneth F.
FAIRLEIGH, Paul
FARNUM, Henry W.
FEBBRARO, Jean-Luc
FELDMAYER, Charles F.
FENIMORE, MG John H
FENNIMAN, James A.
FLAGG, Thomas R.
FLUHR, Edward T.
FLYNN, Mjr Gen Lawrence P.
FOLLERT, Robert P.
FOLLETT, William R.
FORBIS, Mrs. John L.
FORMICOLA, Allison
FORSTER, Nicolas S.
FOUNTAIN, Anthony C.
FOUNTAIN, Gideon
FOUNTAIN, Mrs. John
FOWLER, James L.
FRASER Jr., Colin J,
FRASER, John A.
FRASER, Mrs. Helena
FREEMAN, Dexter
FULRATH Jr., Logan
FULRATH, Adam L.
FULWEILER Jr., John K
FULWEILER Sr., John
FULWEILER, Justin C.
FULWEILER, Mary C.
FULWEILER, Peter C.
FULWEILER, Robinson W.
GALVIN III, John F.
GANDERT, Maj Slade Richard
GENEREUX Jr., BG Paul C.
GENGLER, John
GENGLER, Marion C.
GIGNOUS, Sheilah
GILKES, Mrs. Arthur G.
GILLETTE, Richard
GLAZIER, Virginia C.

GLENDINNING, Meghan
GOETZ, Barbara M.
GOLDSBOROUGH, Nicholas T.
GOODING, Judson
GORDON, Albert H.
GOSHEN M.D., C. Robert
GOWEN II, George W.
GRACE, F Cecil
GRANT-THOROLD, Nicholas
GRANVILLE, Emily L.
GRANVILLE, Mr. Richard C.
GRANVILLE, Mrs. Richard C.
GRANVILLE, Steven C.
GRASKE, Capt Theodore W.
GRASSO, Joseph S.
GREEN, Allen J.
Green, Raymond B.
GREENE, Thurston
GRISWOLD, Tracy Haight
GROSS, Steven F.
GROSSO Jr., E. J.
GRUNEWALD, Raymond
HAAS Jr., George C.
HABER, Warren H.
HAHN, Richard E.
HAIGHT Jr., Sherman P.
HALE, Lt. Paul E.
HALKET, Thomas D.
HALL, Joshua B.
HALL, Leonard C.
HAMEL Jr., Henry E.
HAMMOCK, LTC Gordon R.
HANLEY, LTJG Ret. Robert A.
HANNAN, Anne T.
HARCSAR, Eugene A.
HARGRAVE, Janet Taylor
HARPER, Gordon H.
HARPER, Judith H.
HARRIS, Charles A.
HART, Priscilla
HASKELL III, Robert H.
HATSIS, Mark Anthony
HAYNES, Robert
HAYNES, Schuyler B.

HAYNES, Sophie P-Q
HEALY, Chris
HEALY, Lila R
HEALY, Timothy J.
HEATLEY, Philip O.
HEISKELL, Andrew L.
HERMAN, Theodore L.
HERRING, Mary P.
HEUBSCH, Harriet
HIGGS, John H.
HITE, LTG Ronald
HOAGLAND, Edward M
HOBEN, Michael F
HOCKER, Douglas W.
HOCKING, LCDR James R.
HODENPYL, Mrs. Eugene
HOLBERT, Hayward J.
HOLMES, Robert W.
HOLSOPPLE, Earle T.
HORTON, James B
HOYT, Coleman W.
Hsu, MS Elizabeth R.
HUBBARD, Mrs. Thomas B.
HUBER, Frederick C.
HUGHES, James E.
HUGHES, LTC Micahel
HULL, Terry R.
HUTCHINS, Carol F.
HYATT, Ms Alice H.
HYDE, Capt George W.
IJAMS, W. Seton
IZARD, W. Bolling
JACKS, Kristen M
JACOPOZZI, Alexander
JACOPOZZI, Mrs. Maude
JAFFE, Marc A.
JAFFE, Robert M
JAMES, Philip R.
JEWITT, Joel R. C.
JEWITT, Mrs. David W. P.
JOHNSEY, Walter F.
JOHNSON Jr., Thomas A.
JONES, Christopher H
JONES, Christopher S.

JONES, Mr. David Lloyd
JOSEPH Jr., Anthony
KATINAS, Capt Vincent A
KEATING III, Cletus
KEEFE, Mrs. Arthur T.
KELLY, LTC Kenneth
KEMPER, Claude
KERN, Maj Patrick
KERR III, E. Coe
KERR Jr., Roderick E.
KIERNAN, Nathaniel
KIMTIS, Robert L.
KINARD, Mrs. James P.
KIRCHNER, Karl S. F.
KIRK, Cynthia
KIRKBRIDE, Nicholas L. S.
KISSEL, Michael Case
KLAGES, Constance W.
KLEIN, MG Edward G
KLINCK, Mason J. O.
KLINCKE, Mrs. Gunther
KNIFFIN, Timothy B.
KNUTH, KLAUS
KONDRATIUK, Col. Leonid E.
KORTEA, Richard
KRAUS, Robert M. L.
KRAUSE, Frank E.
KRUEGER, Mrs. H. E.
LA RUE, Mr. David S.
LAINO, Lee
LAKOS, Theodore
LANDSMAN, Bill
LANE, Francis C.
LANIER, Elizabeth K.
LANNON, James D.
LANTERMAN, Col. John V.
LEAHY, Col Peter M.
LEAVEY, Mr. Thomas C.
LEAVEY, Sheila W.
LEAYCRAFT, Matthew
LEISHURE, Hon P. K.
LEON Jr., John M.
LEWIS Jr., Charles W.
LEWIS, Capt. J. Michael
LEWIS, Col. Debra M.
LIEDER, Mrs. Mary A.
LINDH, David E. P.
LINDH, Henry C. B.
LINDLEY, Col. W. Irvin
LIVINGSTON, Lorna M.
LOENING, Albert Palmer
LOENING, Michael
LOHREY, Mary A.
LONG-REED, Mrs. Suzanne
LORENZO, Robert B.
LOUIS, Murray A.
LOVE, Norris
LOVESEY, Kathleen
LUCAS Jr. M.D., Charles C.
LUCAS, LTC James
LUETTERS, Lucia G.
LUNDSTADT, Peter S.
LUNNEY, Capt J. Robert
LUTKINS, Mr. David R.
LYNCH, Robert T.
LYON, William D.
LYONS Jr., Coleman R.
MACCALLUM, Jeffrey W.
MACGUIRE, Schuyler C.
MACKENTY, John E.
MACWILLIE, Col. Donald W.
MADIGAN, Thomas F.
MAGEE, Mary Louise
MALLINSON, James M
MANEE, Monte Stewart
MANNA, Mario A.
MARDEN, Mrs. William G.
MARSHALL Jr., Duncan L.
MARSHALL, Claiborne T.
MARSHALL, T. W.
MARTINEZ Jr., Joseph A.
MASON, Anne M.
MASON, CDR Robert L
MAULL, Ms Diana
MAXWELL, Virginia D.
MCALPIN III, Benjamin B
MCCONNELL, Steven W.
MCGRATH, Thomas J.

MCGUIRE-HUNGRIDGE, Leslie
MCGUNAGLE, G. Patrick
MCILVAINE, Lieghton L.
MCINTOSH, Ann L.
MCLEAN, Linda Durfee
MCLEAN, Margaret
MCLEAN, Robert L.
MEJIA, Luis J.
MELI, Priscilla
MENKEN, Kenneth
MENTZ, Barbara A.
MESTLER, LTC Gilbert E.
MILLER III, Carl N.
MILLER Jr., Philip A.
MISSIRAS, Barbara M.
MISSIRAS, Dr. Michael
MOGER, Dr. Claudina F.
MONKS, Shawn
MONTOMERY, Franklin W.
MOORE, Arthur
MOREL, Barbara P.
MORGAN, Eleanor
MORGULAS, Seth
MORRISON Jr., James C.
MORRISON, Carol
MORRISSEY, Thomas J.
MUNTON DDS, William V.
MUR, Raphael
MURNANE III, George
NADEL, Dr. Robert S.
NASH, Capt. John F.
NAUNHEIM, Alfred R.
NAVAL OFFICER'S CLUB
NEILL, Michael S. Del
NELSON II, Norman F.
NEPHEW, Robert M.
NESBITT, Micahel M.
NEUHOFF, Roger A.
NEUWIRTH, Mr. Francis
NICHOLAIS, Michael A,
NICHOLS, David H.
NICKERSON, Miss Mary
NICKERSON, Richard K.
NOBLE, William L.

NOFI, Mr. Albert
NOYES, Jose W.
NUTT, Robert L.
NUTT, Stanley B.
O'BUCKLEY, Gerald T.
O'CONNELL, Charles J.
O'CONNELL, Helen
O'CONNOR, Richard W.
O'KEEFE, Eric
O'MALLEY, John Arthur
O'PRAY, Mr. Bruce
O'ROURKE, Richard T.
OLBERG, Forbes
OLMSTED, Mrs. Joseph N.
OLSEN, Mrs. Martin A.
OLSON, Douglas L.
OLSON, Dr. Ralph A.
OSBORNE, Rev Martin J.
OSMOLOVSKY, Sharon
OTTO, Ann M.
PACAUD, C. E.
PACE, Eric
PACKARD, Thomas W.
PACKSHAW, Capt. Justin
PAGEL, Alex B.
PALMER, Jennifer
PALMER, Lucius Noyes
PALMER, Mrs. Stephen
PARRY, Rawdon
PAYNE, John W.
PERSON, John C.
PETERSON, CDR Harry
PETERSON, Col. James C.
PHELAN, Rev Thomas
PHILBRICK, Barbara
PHILIP, Peter V. N.
PICKERING Jr., F. B.
PICKERING, Roxana B.
PICKERING, Timothy
PICOTT, James S. G.
PINE, Roswell Dean
PIOVARCY, Lee L.
PITCHER, Stephen
PLATT, Mr. Frank C.

SQUADRON A

PLUNKET, The Hon Shaun
POCHNA, Peter
POINDEXTER, John B.
POTTER, Delcour S.
POTTER, H. David
POWELL, Harry G.
POWELL, Mr. David W.
POWELL, Peter I. A.
PRAY Jr., Malcolm S.
PROUT, William
PROWELL, Mrs. Ricahrd
PUTNAM, Mrs. Harrington
RAFF, Bridget
RAFF, Mr. Peter K.
RAFF, Nancy W.
RALSTON, Mr. Robert G.
RASMUSSEN, Howard L.
RASSIAS, Cecily
RASSIAS, John Nicholas
READ, Mrs. Barclay K.
REBOUL, Edward L.
REBOUL, Mr. John W.
REILLY, John J
REILLY, Robert R.
RENTSCHLER, Col. George A.
RIBLE, Capt, Stephen V.
RICHARDS, Mrs. Benjamin R.
RICHARDS, William B.
RITTENHOUSE, Valerie W.
RITZ, Frederick W.
RIVKIN, James
ROBERSON, Robert S.
ROBINSON, MGEN Gwynn H.
ROGERS, Grant
ROGERS, Peter H.
ROSE, MG Robert
ROSS, Christopher B.
ROSS, Edward H.
ROSS, Sarane H.
RUSSELL, Hollis F.
RUSSO, Thomas A.
SAMUELSON, Kjell
SANDS, Harold W.
SANDS-PINGOT, Col. Guy

SCHAFF, David
SCHAUFFLER, Frederick A.
SCHAUFFLER, Nancy A.
SCHIEFFELIN, Timothy
SCHIFF III, William
SCHIFF, Lt. Terry
SCHNEIDAU, Frances C.
SCHNEIDER, Col. Paul A.
SCHNEIDER, Kurt J.
SCHOEPFER, James W.
SCHOLL, Jerome T.
SCHWARZKOPF, Gen. H. Norman
SEITER, Stephen R.
SEMAN III, George C.
SENN, Karl A.
SEYMOUR, Col. Nicholas D. A.
SHANNON Jr., Mr. Jack H.
SHANNON, William H
SHARPE, Mrs. Elly Peet
SHARRETTS Jr., Edward P.
SHARRETTS, A. Bret
SHAW, James T.
SHERIDAN, Virginia G.
SHERMAN, Wendy
SHERWOOD, Scott L.
SHIRK, Francis G.
SIEGFRIED, Robert E.
SIKORSKI, Robert S.
SIMM, David E.
SIMPSON, Alison
SIMPSON, H. Lynn
SIMPSON, William K.
SINCLAIR, CW3 Thomas J.
SINNOTT, John P.
SKIDMORE, Philip M.
SKOMAL, Bernard J.
SKOMAL, Lenore M.
SKOMAL, Magda K.
SKOMAL, Martin
SLATER, Stuart
SLOAN, David R.
SMETHURST, Alejandra
SMETHURST, William
SMITH Jr., James P.

SMITH, David M.
SMITH, Frederick B.
SMITH, Mrs. Emelie B.
SMITH, Roger S.
SMITH, Ryan D.
SMITH, Winthrop D.
SNYDER, Richard P.
SOLLECITO, Daniel V.
SPRAGUE, Kurth
SQUADRON A ASSN INC.
STABLER, Hon. Wells
STAELIN, John R.
STANIFORD, Daniel A.
STANTON, Christina,
STARK, L. James
STARK, louis B.
STEBBINS, James F.
STEGMAN Jr., William A.
STETTINIUS, Edward T.
STETZER, Susanne
STEVENS, Barrett W.
STODDARD, Gracey
STOKES III, Francis J.
STONE, Maj. George H.
STOUT, Franklin C.
STOVEKEN, James
STRANG, J. P.
STRASSGUETL, Jane S. G.
STRONG, Sally B.
STUART, Bruce
STUHR, Bernard C.
SUES, Mr. John M.
SULLIVAN, Eugene C.
SWEENY, Mrs. Bradley P.
SWEET, Audrey M. S.
SWIACKI, Jeanne G.
SWINDELL, Capt. Samuel V. S.
SYNAN, Rev. Thomas
TAGGART, Don B.
TAGGART, Douglas D.
TAGGART, Mrs. John V.
TALBOTT, Rev. John J.
TAYLOR IV, John W.
TCHEREPNINE, Peter

TEEGER, John L.
TERRY, Ward
THERKILDSEN, Alfred
THOMAS, Joseph Michael
THOMPSON, Earle J.
THORS, Jane
THROWER, Mitch
TIEDEMEANN Jr., Barrie
TIPA, Col. Ronald J.
TOBIN, Mrs. Sarah
TOMPKINS, Frederic
TOWNSEND, David D.
TRAFELET, Remy W.
TRIPP, James D.
TROMMERS, Kenneth A.
TURINO Jr., William G.
TURNER, Albert C.
TURNER, Charles F. C.
TWISS Jr., John R.
TWISS, John S
TWISS, Mr. Donald
TWISS, Russell W.
UPJOHN, Charles D.
VAN BERGEN, J. F. A.
VAN SINDEREN Jr., Adrian
VELLON, Kenneth
VERDI, Philips
VINES, LTC Walter F.
VOLK, Austin N.
VON HASSELL, Agostino
VON HEISERMAN, Julian
VOORHEES, Natalie R.
VOORHEES, Willard P. V.
VOORHIS, H. M. Baird
WAGNER, Jerald F.
WALDNER, J. Dudley
WALKER II, Samuel R.
WALKER Jr., William C.
WALKER, William
WALLACE, Robert
WARD, MGEN William F
WARRINER, Donald S.
WASSMAN, E. Robert
WATSON, Maj. Maurice

WEIHS, George J.
WEIHS, George P.
WELLING, W. Lambert
WELLS, Peter S.
WEMYSS, Marie
WHALEN, Col. James F.
WHELAN Jr., Sidney S.
WHITE, Patricia S.
WHITEHOUSE Sr., William F.
WHITLOW, Elizabeth J.
WHITLOW, Robert S.
WHITNEY DVM., William H.
WHITNEY Jr., Robert U.
WHITNEY, Charles T.
WHITNEY, Joseph C.
WILCHINSKY, Victoria S.
WILCOX, Gordon Cumnock
WILDER, David St. Clair
WILLIAMSON, Constance
WILSON, John J.
WINN, Michael P. A.
WINSLOW, John Grenville
WINZINGER Sr., Gen. Robert J.
WISTER, W. David
WITTER, Michael D.
WOOD, John H.
WOOLVERTON, Arthur R.
WOOLVERTON, Charles B.
WOOLVERTON, John
WORTH, Douglas C.
WRANGEL, Dr. Christine
WRIGHT III, William P.
WRIGHT III., Mrs William P.
WRIGHT IV, William P.
WRIGHT, Elizabeth
WUTT, Mark R.
WYLIE, Robert S.
YEAGER, Ms Jill T.
YOUNG, CAROL C.
YOUNG, David B.
YOURY, Robert S.
ZELLE, Kent N.
ZIMMERMAN, Arthur A.
ZITO, Rovert J. A.

2004 OFFICERS

Robert U. Whitney, Jr.	Chairman, Board of Governors
Robert L. McLean	President
Benjamin B. McAlpin, III	Vice-President
George A. Rentschler	Vice-President
Logan Fulrath, Jr.	Secretary/Judge Advocate
Michael David Witter	Treasurer

EXECUTIVE DIRECTOR
Harriet Huebsch

CHAPLAIN
The Rev. James L. Burns
The Rev. Thomas Synan

COMMITTEES

EXECUTIVE COMMITTEE
Benjamin B. McAlpin, Chairman

John L. Adams
Arthur Armitage
Samuel N. Benjamin
Henry L. Collins, III
George J. Dotsey

Charles A. Harris
Vincent A. Katinas
Edward G. Klein
Michael David Witter

Emeritus: James B. Horton
Louis B. Stark

ARCHIVES COMMITTEE
George J. Dotsey

HISTORICAL COMMITTEE
Vincent A. Katinas, Chairman

INVESTMENT COMMITTEE
Robert L. McLean, Chairman

SQUADRON A

MEMBERSHIP DEVELOPMENT COMMITTEE
Michael D. Witter, Chairman

NOMINATING COMMITTEE
Kent Coughlin, Chairman

SQUADRON A FOUNDATION COMMITTEE
Robert U. Whitney, Chairman

SQUADRON A FUND COMMITTEE
Henry L. Collins, III, Chairman

BOARD OF GOVERNORS

To serve until 2005:
    Kent Coughlin
    John Galvin, III
    George W. Gowen, III
    James B. Horton
    Vincent A. Katinas
    David Nichols
    James Morrison
    Ralph A. Olson
    Donald Twiss
    J. Dudley Waldner

To serve until 2006:
    Samuel N. Benjamin
    Stewart Brown
    Garrett Bowden
    Lawrence Flynn
    Charles Harris
    Michael Hoben
    Philip R. James
    Peter Leisure
    Kenneth Trommers
    Robert Winzinger

To serve until 2007:
    Emanuel Amatrudo
    Arthur L. Armitage
    Patrick J. Brennan
    Thomas Britton
    Stehen Dorr
    George J. Dotsey
    Christopher S. Jones
    Francis Shirk
    Daniel Staniford
    Peter Tcherepnine

To serve until 2008:
    Edward Bimberg
    Alexander Cannon
    Henry Collins, III
    James Fenniman
    Gideon Fountain
    Duncan L. Marshall
    David Powell
    Irwin "Pete" Powell
    Christopher Ross
    William Smethurst

To serve until 2009:
    John L. Adams
    Robert Ballard
    George Barker
    Alfred Bisset
    Lance Bondy
    Robert Follert
    Edward G. Klein
    Frederick Pickering, Jr
    Peter Raff
    William Ward

2004 GOVERNORS DINNER.
COLONEL BOB MCLEAN, PRESIDENT; MG RICHARD COLT, COMMANDER 77TH REGIONAL SUPPORT COMMAND, SPEAKER;
MR. ROBERT WHITNEY, CHAIRMAN; MR. LOGAN FULRATH, SECRETARY.

SQUADRON A

ADDENDUM

By

Robert L. McLean

Eleemosynary Activities

The Squadron A Fund was created to support horse related activities with money raised by the sale of a Remington statue. The New York Community Trust manages the fund. The organizations which have received financial assistance include the U.S. Cavalry Association, the 101st Cavalry Museum, the West Point Equestrian Team, the National Horse Sports Foundation, the ASPCA, the American Horse Protection Association and several therapeutic riding organizations including Windrush Farm, Pegasus, Winslow Therapeutic and North American Riding.

The Squadron A Foundation was created to support a wider range of worthy causes, emphasizing the military and cavalry. In particular, the Foundation provides five $500 scholarships annually to soldiers of the 101st Cavalry. The Commander told us that there could not be a better expression of recognition and continuity for the unit. It shows that the veterans really care, it is great for morale and the money is much needed. Last year, the awards made very visible impact as they were presented at summer camp after some very successful firing exercises. We also purchased a video camera for them to record activities at Ground Zero. In addition, we provided a Thanksgiving dinner for the unit and their families at Fort Hamilton. Keeping involved in their activities is very important to both organizations.

Financial support was needed in the 1980s by two of our associated clubs. As clubs don't qualify for charitable contributions, we assisted the Cavalry and Guards Club in London directly from our treasury. Their 100-year leasehold was coming due and they needed to raise money to pay for it or otherwise lose the building. The executive committee felt that the relationship between the two clubs was so important that a gift of $10,000 was made from the Squadron A Association treasury. In addition, another $10,000 was donated to them by individual contributions from our membership. In the second case, the Women's National Republican Club had a short-term cash flow problem when our treasury was low. One of our members provided a personal loan of $10,000, which was subsequently repaid.

A Navy Seal informed us, after having returned from Iraq, that U.S. Army Engineers had done a great job of building schools but lacked school supplies. Vince Katinis had a solution. In his business, he knows several manufacturers of promotional materials who make everything from ballpoint pens to Frisbees. Often, many are unsaleable because of a misspelling or typographical error, but nevertheless very usable. He asked his friends to donate the goods, which they did. Also, some members made Squadron A Foundation contributions for the cause and a very worthwhile shipment was assembled and sent to Iraq.

Creation of Associate Membership

After the draft was abolished, it became unpopular for most young people to enter the military service voluntarily. The result would clearly be a shortage of veterans wanting to become squadron members. To accommodate all the many friends of the military, who had not actually served, we created Associate Memberships, which eliminated the requirement of prior service.

Haberdashery

The following items all of exceptional quality and very reasonably priced, are available to Squadron A members. Member Ken Trommers, then the head of J. Press advised on the selections and sources.

Included are silk ties, bow ties, cummerbunds, blazer patches with sabers logo, secretary type wallet in leather with Squadron A silk, navy and gold striped six-foot woolen scarf, blazer buttons and double old-fashioned glasses with crossed sabers insignia.

New Events

Traditionally, Squadron A has a great Christmas Party, Squadron A Day at the races at Belmont and a beautiful Memorial Service at the Church of the Heavenly Rest followed by a reception at the Leash. We also had some great parties aboard the aircraft carrier U.S.S. *Intrepid*. The National Horse Show, before it left New York, was a favorite Squadron A event for decades.

We have experimented with many new events and have some, which are now attended annually as follows:

West Point Equestrian Team Collegiate Match at West Point (Squadron A tent), Long Island Wyandanch Club Shoots, Fall; sporting clays Winter; Tower Shoot Sotheby's Sports Art Cocktail Party

> Harrison Cup Polo – Yale vs. Virginia in Connecticut
> All Club New Years Eve Party
> Military Order of Foreign Wars President's Day Celebration

Special Events have included harness races at Yonkers Raceway, ocean fishing, golf at West Point, weapons firing at the 101st Cavalry Armory, Veterans Corps of Artillery Military Ball at the Yale Club, shooting of the M-1 tank and the M-2 Bradley fighting vehicle at Aberdeen Proving Ground and a West Point football game.

In the interest of stimulating new membership, we have created four informal parties each year with cocktails at 6pm for one half hour followed by brief remarks by a dignitary. The parties occur after Executive Committee meetings so that everyone can mingle and discover more about Squadron A. Michael Witter has volunteered to try to recruit younger members and has been very successful in attracting many candidates. The dignitaries so far have been:

LTC Mario Costagliola	Commander, 101st Cavalry
Chris Jones	Commentator, FOX News
Captain Drew Bisset	Navy Seal (Back from Iraq)
Alfred Bisset	Pres. A. G. Bisset, Currency Experts
Col. Nick Seymour UK	UN Peacekeeping Officer

New Honorary Members
   Vice President Richard Cheney
   General H. Norman Schwarzkopf
   General Gordon Sullivan
   Major General Donald Campbell
   Major General William Collins
   Major General John H. Fenimore
   Major General Richard S. Colt

Reciprocal Clubs

Reciprocal Club arrangements are a very attractive feature of Squadron A membership. Our member, David Powell makes a hobby of knowing about them. With his help, we have been able to establish reciprocity with several clubs. Kindly, the Women's National Republican Club has given us the privilege of using their reciprocals as Associate Members. A list of the reciprocal clubs follows:

SQUADRON A

Bath and County Club, Bath England
The Cavalry and Guards Club, London, England
City Club, Baton Rouge, Louisiana
City University Club, London, England
Pinnacle Club (formerly Denver Petroleum), Denver, Colorado
Soldiers, Sailors & Airmen's Club, 36th St & Lexington Ave., New York City, NY
Tennis & Racquet Club (no overnight rooms), Boston, Mass.
University Club of San Francisco, San Francisco, California
The Royal Hamilton Amateur Dinghy Club, Hamilton, Bermuda

WNRC – UNITED STATES

The Argyle Hotel, Los Angeles, California
The Arizona Club (no rooms), Phoenix, Arizona
Berkeley City Club, Berkeley, California 94704
California Yacht Club, Marina Del Rey, California
Capitol Hill Club (no rooms), Washington, DC
The College Club, Boston, Mass.
Denver Athletic Club (no rooms), Denver, Colorado
Intown Club (no rooms), Cleveland, Ohio
Los Angeles Athletic Club, Los Angeles, California

The Riviera Tennis and Country Club, Pacific Palisades, California
The Surf Club, Surfside, Florida
Women's City Club (Union Club), Boston, Mass.

WNRC – ABROAD
Cercle de L'Union inter Alliee (no rooms), Paris, France
The Chelsea Club (no rooms), Ottawa, Canada
The Georgian Club, Vancouver, BC, Canada
International Club (no rooms), Brussels, Belgium
Club Portugese, Porto, Portugal
Schlosshotel Korssberg, Kromeberg, Germany
The Sloane Club, London, England
The St. James Club, Antigua, West Indies
The St. James Club, London, United Kingdom
The St. James Club, Paris, France
University Women's Club, London, England
University Women's Club of Montreal (Union Club), Montreal, Canada

A letter of introduction must be obtained from the Squadron A office for each and every visit to any reciprocal club. Rules for each club regarding dress, children, etc. must e observed.

Dues

The management of Association funds has yielded excellent returns. As a result, the Squadron A Executive Committee has voted every year since 1985 to hold the dues constant and to subsidize deficits. It is felt that the policy has helped to keep our loyal members intact and to attract new members. Our membership has been increasing and we have been able to find many people with the same values as have been traditional with Squadron troopers.

Increasing Tempo of National Guard and Reserve Deployments

In the Korean, Vietnam and Cold Wars there were virtually no call-ups of the guard and reserves. Since the beginning of the first Gulf War in 1990, things have changed dramatically.

At that time, the 101st Cavalry was called to active duty to help train Regular Army forces. They deployed to the National Training Center at Fort Irwin, California to serve with the Regular Army 32nd

Guards Motorized Rifle Regiment as an aggressor force to train the 155th Armored Brigade. The colonel of the regiment awarded them the Certificate of Achievement for outstanding performance. He remarked, "Laboring under extreme conditions for both men and equipment, the Squadron worked tirelessly, successfully meeting all mission requirements. The professional dedication of the 101st significantly aided the 32nd to effectively train the 155th Armored Brigade. This outstanding effort is indicative of a total dedication to excellence on the part of the combat infantry and is worthy of the highest Regimental accolade for a tough job well done. The performance of these soldiers reflects great credit upon the 1st Squadron, 101st Cavalry, and the United States Army." The Department of the Army also officially commended the 101st Cavalry for extraordinary meritorious service. The award is included herewith.

Two Squadron members had key roles in Operation Desert Storm. Major General Barker was the Assistant Deputy Chief of Staff Personnel Department of the Army for Mobilization and Reserve Affairs where he was responsible for Reserve and National Guard matters. Major General Donald Campbell commanded the 353rd Civil Affairs Command as the senior officer in Northern Iraq. His mission was protecting the Kurds from violence, which continued after the war had ended.

Major General Edward Klein, a Squadron A Governor, was the Commander of the New York National Guard in the late 1990s. At that time, 1,000 of his soldiers were deployed in Bosnia. Therefore, he served on active duty to visit them and to find ways to help them and to provide what they needed to accomplish their various missions.

As a former Commander of the 101st Cavalry, he recently informed me that they have been officially designated to participate in the Partners for Peace program. The idea is to have the best National Guard units aid and advise various foreign countries. Many countries have no standing army and so the meeting of the minds between respective guard people is very favorable. The 101st has been assigned to help Albania. They have already had good meetings and their counterparts will be coming to the U.S. for additional consultation.

Reflecting on the foregoing, it is easy to see why "An Army of One" name was created. Due to cost cutting after the end of the Cold War, the Regular Army was stripped of personnel in most support activities such as Medical, Medical Service, Engineers, Civil Affairs, Public Affairs, Military Police, Ordnance, Transportation and Quartermaster amongst others. As a result, any conflict results in the call-up of Guard and Reserve personnel who provide those services and of course the combat arms soldiers.

As we write, the 101st Cavalry has been deployed to Iraq under the 42nd Infantry Division. They were told to leave their tanks at home and were provided infantry and civil disturbance training. They will be mechanized with HUMVEES. Former Commanders of the 101st, Col. Mario Costagliola is the G-3 (Plans and Operations) and Brigadier General Paul Genereaux is Assistant Division Commander of the 42nd Infantry Division. Squadron A is coordinating with the leader of their family group to find ways of providing help where needed.

Conclusion

Squadron A, now called the 101st Cavalry, has provided protection to New York City, soldiers for many wars for 115 years from 1889 to 2004, great social and horse related activities and in the recent past has added clubhouse privileges, many more reciprocal club arrangements and new events. Over the years, we have weathered many changes, but continue to excel as the only military related club with clubhouse rooms and facilities located in New York City. We are planning to be around for a very long time and hope that future generations will capture the spirit of Squadron A.

DEPARTMENT OF THE ARMY

TO ALL WHO SHALL SEE THESE PRESENTS, GREETING:

THIS IS TO CERTIFY THAT

1st Squadron, 101st Cavalry
New York Army National Guard

IS OFFICIALLY COMMENDED

FOR

EXTRAORDINARY MERITORIOUS SERVICE

**IN SUPPORT OF
OPERATION DESERT STORM**

1990 - 1991

The "Dickey Bird" Insignia

Squadron A Trooper with Guidon